A DOG OWNER'S GUIDE TO

THE ROTTWEILER

Tetra⦿Press

No. 16028

A DOG OWNER'S GUIDE TO

THE ROTTWEILER

Joan Blackmore
Photographs by Marc Henrie

A Salamander Book

©1987 Salamander Books Ltd.,
Published in the USA by
Tetra Press,
3001 Commerce Street,
Blacksburg,
VA 24060.

ISBN 1-56465-122-3

Library of Congress Number: 87-050043

Credits

Editor: Tony Hall   Designer: Glynis Edwards
Photographs: Marc Henrie, Tylla Berger (pp 18, 19), Artur Gallas (pp 15,
19), Mary Macphail (pp 21), Sinclair Stammers/Science Photo Lib. (pp.
95).
Illustrations: Ray Hutchins
Color origination: Rodney Howe Ltd
Typesetting: AKM Associates (UK) Ltd. The Old Mill
Printed in Belgium

Contents

Foreword

I first met Joan Blackmore about 20 years ago in London, with her
Rottweiler, Panzer. I was fascinated how many tricks this remarkable
dog could do, and I thought how well Joan had trained him.
    When Joan asked me to write a foreword for this book, I was
delighted to do so. With this book, Joan passes on her years of
experience with dogs. Whether you are buying your first Rottweiler, or
whether you are breeding for the first time, or even if you are an
expert, believe me, there is something of interest for everyone. You
will feel Joan's unlimited love and understanding for our Rottweilers.
This book will help you to train your Rottweiler into a self-confident
friend and guard-dog which will look after your house and family.
Joan, thank you for this book.

Tylla Berger

*Mrs Berger is the widow of Freidrich Berger, for many years the Chief
Breed Warden for Rottweilers in West Germany.*

Author

Joan Blackmore has been working with dogs all her life. She owned her first dog – a Bull Terrier – at 11 years of age, and nine years later qualified another Bull Terrier CDX at working trials. Joan bred, showed and trained Bull Terriers until 1963, when she began her long and successful association with Rottweilers. Her first Rottweiler Emil Blackforest (Panzer), under her tutelage, also qualified for the coveted CDX.

Joan is a past-President and currently Chairman of the Rottweiler Club of Great Britain. She is a show judge of international standing and judged Rottweilers at Crufts' in 1982. Joan has imported six German Rottweilers into Britain over the years, including Bulli v.d. Waldequelle. As well as breeding and judging her Rottweilers, Joan is also an extremely successful trainer of dogs for film and television with over 3000 parts credited over the past 23 years.

Veterinary Consultant

Keith Butt, MA, VetMB(Cantab), MRCVS qualified in 1961 at Cambridge University. He runs his own veterinary practice in Kensington, London, and is himself a breeder and owner of many different breeds of pedigree dogs.

US Consultant

Hal Sundstrom, as president of Halamar Inc, publishers, of North Virginia, has been editing and publishing magazines on travel and pure-bred dogs since 1972. He is the recipient of six national writing and public excellence awards from the Dog Writer's Association of America, of which he is now president, and he is a past president of Collie Club of America.

Hal has an extensive background and enormous experience in the dog world as a breeder/handler/exhibitor, match and sweeps judge, officer and director of specialty and all-breed clubs, show and symposium chairman, and officer of the Arizona and Hawaii Councils of Dog Clubs.

Photographer

Marc Henrie began his career as a Stills man at the famous Ealing Film Studios in London. He then moved to Hollywood where he worked for MGM, RKO, Paramount and Warner Brothers.

After he had returned to England, Marc specialized in photographing dogs and cats, establishing an international reputation.

He has won numerous photographic awards, most recently the Kodak Award for the Best Animal Photograph and the Neal Foundation Award for Outstanding Photography of Animal Behaviour.

Marc is married to ex-ballet dancer, Fiona Henrie. They live in West London with their daughter Fleur, two King Charles Cavalier Spaniels and a cat called Topaz.

Author's acknowledgements

The author wishes to thank Annette Colbourne, Violet Slade and Jane and Michael Heath for allowing their dogs to be photographed; Tylla Berger and Artur Gallas of Dortmund for their invaluable help in West Germany; Mary Macphail for her support; all the Blackmore, Murphy and Dean families and last but not least Molly Redman for typing the manuscript.

Introduction

Is the Rottweiler for you?

The Rottweiler is a very interesting and rewarding dog – but only for certain types of human temperament. The powerful frame and equally powerful mind of this breed is not to be taken on without a lot of thought and a real interest in the dog itself.

The males can reach up to 27in (69cm) at the shoulder and can weigh over 125lb (57kg), so with a breed like this you must be sure that you have the dog under control at all times and insist that it uses its mind and strength for you and not against you. A Rottweiler on your side is a wonderful animal, a Rottweiler working against you is the exact opposite.

This breed is also expensive to maintain. They need good quality food and have large appetites, so keep this firmly in mind: be sure that you can afford to feed and house such a large dog, and that you have a suitable, well-fenced garden or yard.

Nervous people looking for a cheap burglar alarm will find it better to consult a firm of security lock specialists, since an untrained Rottweiler can do a lot more damage to your home than the average burglar!

Equally, the young macho male looking for an accessory to his tough image, and encouraging a young Rottweiler to roar at all and sundry, will soon find himself in court and the luckless dog could easily have a destruction order slapped on it.

People looking for a dog to chain in their yard to deter wrongdoers could also find themselves in trouble with a Rottweiler as, unloved and untrained, the dog will at best howl loudly in loneliness and despair and, at worst, bite the person inflicting this terrible suffering!

What type of person should have a Rottweiler?

(a) The owner should be ready to teach the dog all the basic things it needs to know;

(b) should be prepared to make the dog part of the family unit, subject to all the rules imposed by the average family;

(c) must have a sense of fair play, a sense of humour and the ability to make pleasure or displeasure felt very keenly by the dog;

(d) should make sure that all members of the family love, respect and want the dog as much as he or she does, and are prepared to be as firm and fair to the dog as he or she is, with one member of the family at home all day.

Having said all this, the Rottweiler in a good environment is a joy to own; when nothing is happening the Rottweiler sleeps, but when danger threatens the dog is ready and willing to face it. When you want to play, your Rottweiler is eager to join in the game. This breed is not given to senseless barking – when the Rottweiler barks, go and look, as there is usually a good reason. If you like love and cuddles, your macho Rottweiler loves them too, for they have a very soft heart with the family and friends.

Some members of this breed are 'growlers' – that is to say, they grumble in a friendly way when their back is rubbed. It is almost a way of 'talking' their pleasure. Some Rottweilers, on the other hand, hate over-familiarity by strangers, especially the 'all dogs love me' types who grab a dog roughly and slap it about in a supposedly friendly way. If you see your Rottweiler in this situation, step in and tell the offending person to stop. The dog will tell you of his anger by going very still, and a very 'black' expression will come into his eyes. That is the point when, unless the offender stops, the dog will make his dislike of such treatment felt! I must stress that not all Rottweilers do this, but it is as well to

Left: *Rottweilers are happiest when they are included in all aspects of family life.*

Below: *If you can train, feed and house a Rottweiler well, you will have an invaluable companion.*

11

know that some do, and be warned. It is not easy to tell friends to leave your dog alone, but to own a Rottweiler you have to be as honest and tough as the dogs themselves.

This breed is a working dog and, although they do not make you feel like the world's best dog trainer as do some of the shepherd breeds, once trained they still retain their pride and are very seldom slavish. They are more likely to assume the role of a good mate.

Generally speaking, the Rottweiler loves his home and family and has little desire to stray off. I have only known four Rottweilers who strayed, and they all lived on large country estates with no perimeter visible to them, and all were left to their own devices for hours. With no guidance or 'lines' which must not be crossed, they were unable to recognize the rules.

The Rottweiler in society

Children and Rottweilers get on well, providing the owner is a good referee. Rebuke the child who is misbehaving with the dog, and vice versa: both must learn to respect the other! I only know one Rottweiler who has bitten a child; the dog was provoked by having an ice lolly stick poked into his rectum and he gave the child a nip with jaws that could have broken the child's arm. The dog was subsequently re-homed in a family with three delightful children and he lived happily until he died, with no problems at all.

Left: *In show position, the champion Rottweiler at Crufts' 1987, CH. Aylsham Beauty of Potterspride.*

Above: *Another aspect of owning a Rottweiler is carting; made possible by the breed's strength and will to work.*

If you wish to have your dog accept cats, horses, cattle, sheep and other dogs, you must introduce them from an early age and very sternly rebuke the dog for any chasing or worrying. It is essential that you have the strength of character to insist on perfect behaviour; you will find that you will get acceptance if you demand that your dog conforms to high standards of obedience. A wishy-washy approach will fail to bring out the best in the Rottweiler. This, obviously, applies to all training.

Males of this breed can be very aggressive with other dogs. It is as well to anticipate this, and deal with the dog very firmly the first time he tries it on. There is nothing nicer than a male Rottweiler which has enough self confidence and training to totally ignore other dogs in any situation, and nothing worse than one which wants to bully every other dog. It is up to the owner to make it clear that such behaviour will not be tolerated.

The Rottweiler is a very special dog: a well-trained member of this breed is a constant delight and popular with everyone, whereas the misunderstood, untrained or thoroughly spoilt Rottweiler is a disgrace to the breed at best and, at worst, is a menace and may need to be put down.

Above: *An example of a long-haired Rottweiler. Note the hairy fringing on the ears, chest and back of legs.*

Right: *Blitz, owned and trained by Artur Gallas of Dortmund. This was originally a problem dog before training.*

So remember, a dog is what you make it, by training or environment or upbringing, call it what you will. If you do not have the time or the patience to socialize and teach your dog, then please do not buy a Rottweiler as this is not the breed for you. I see many so-called 'problem dogs' during the course of my work, and 99 per cent of them are simply ill-educated or misunderstood. Once the owners realize why their dog behaves as it does, then one can begin to teach them remedial procedures. Sadly, some owners are just not capable of teaching their dog.

This breed is not for ignorant, unperceptive, non-positive people. Rottweiler owners *must* be able to react in a positive way to be clear in their training methods, to be fun but fair and firm. They need to be hard enough to administer punishment when necessary, in a swift but effective way, but equally quick to praise and love when the dog has behaved correctly. So that he is in no doubt as to what is the right conduct.

The results of neglect

Due to the recent increase in demand for these dogs, many Rottweilers are being bred from untypical, un-X-rayed (to check for hip dysplasia) and bad temperamented parents, mainly due to greed or ignorance. Many people are neglectful when they breed a litter, selling pups to just anyone; later on, the pups, in their turn, get bred from, un-X-rayed, often to 'Fred' down the road who is also un-X-rayed but is said to be a 'lovely big dog' as though great size were a breed feature. In fact, oversized Rottweilers usually die earlier, are more prone to lameness for various reasons, and are often too slow to do a good day's work. So, in just a few generations have come litters of potential cripples looking vaguely like real Rottweilers, being sold for a pittance and ending up in dog homes all over the country. I can see no merit at all in the fact that over 5000 Rottweiler puppies were registered in Britain in 1986, or that over 2400 Rottweilers were registered in the USA in December 1986 alone!

If you are thinking of buying a Rottweiler, please re-read this chapter and also carefully consider the next chapter before deciding honestly if this dog is for you. If your decision is 'yes', then I hope that you will choose carefully, rear lavishly, train thoroughly and love mightily, and you will enjoy one of the most rewarding experiences a dog can give.

Chapter One

A HISTORY OF THE BREED

The origins
The Rottweiler of legend
The A.D.R.K.

THE ORIGINS

The Rottweiler's origins go back to Roman times. When the mighty legions marched long distances to do battle, they had no refrigerated trucks, or cans of bully beef, so supplies had to be live, on the hoof. Hardy, powerful dogs were needed to control the herds of cattle and a dog very much like the Rottweiler was used; it may not have been the black and tan standard type, but our dogs today carry this tenacious and brave heritage. For those dogs were brave, having to deal with cattle which were probably not as placid as the average milking cow today. The herds had to be protected from marauding wolves or even cattle rustlers, the treks were arduous routes across mountains and rivers, heat and intense cold had to be borne with equal fortitude. At the end of the march these dogs would defend their masters in battle with great courage.

In those times, wounds would either get better or the man and his dog would die. There were no drugs, no hospitals, so they had to be tough to survive. Little packs of these dogs would sometimes be left behind, and in the small town of Rottweil, which was once a Roman settlement and is now part of West Germany, they became popular as local cattle-herding dogs. Nestling on the banks of the Neckar River, Rottweil was a market town, to which farmers would bring herds for sale, using their dogs to halve the work.

There is a nice little story which tells of farmers getting drunk on the proceeds of a good day's business, but first tying their bags of gold around the necks of the dogs to ensure the safety of their money. True or false we shall never know, but it has gone down as legend.

When the railroads came and the movement of cattle by road over long distances was banned

Top: Ralph v. Neckar, 1907 Note the long back and muzzle, the lack of substance, the shoulder and reachy neck.

Below centre: Jack v. Schifferstadt. The dog is now showing more substance, with a stronger head and top line.

by law, the Rottweiler was out of a job. Some people used them to pull carts full of produce, but their main task was denied them. For a time the dogs which had been called Metzgerhunde (butcher's dog) were ignored. Numbers declined, until in 1905 there was only one bitch left in

Bottom left: *Seiglinde v.d. Steinlach. A bitch with a strong head and good top line.*

Above: *Leo v. Cannstatt. Note how the head is improving and good body is coming through.*

Below: *International Champion Hexe v. Marchenwald, 1977. Sister to UK and US champions.*

Rottweil itself, though elsewhere the breed had survived. Matters were improving, however. In 1899 the first breed club was formed under the title: 'The International Club for Leonberger and Rottweiler Dogs'. This unfortunately did not survive for very long and it was not until 1907 that the breed finally got the organization it deserved with the formation of The German Rottweiler Club in Heidelberg. This was the first club to organize Rottweiler breeding systematically. About ten years later in 1910, the breed became recognized as a service dog, capable of police and army duties, and from that time onwards this breed went from strength to strength.

THE ROTTWEILER OF LEGEND

Another story, from the time of Kaiser Wilhelm II, was about a policeman and his Rottweiler in Kiel. The pair were sent off to sort out a fight in a tavern where a large number of drunken sailors were really going to town. The policeman and his dog went in, restored peace, made several arrests and escorted the prisoners back to the jail. Apparently, when the Kaiser

heard about the incident, he expressed a wish to meet the policeman and his police dog. Before the Kaiser could shake the hand of the hero it was required that the policeman remove his helmet to signal to his Rottweiler that he was 'off duty' before anyone could touch him.

The sterling qualities of this breed made it a good war dog, too, especially for patrolling areas where silence was essential. Some breeds get excited, whining and barking when taken out to work; not the Rottweiler, which calmly goes ahead doing the job with the minimum of fuss and dealing with any wrongdoers in the same strong, efficient way.

I once spoke to a man who was 'taken' by a Rottweiler patrol dog during the last war. The man was desperate to escape and stabbed the dog with a knife, but the dog hung on and though both were bleeding profusely, it would not let him go until the handler came and called 'Aus' (out), whereupon the dog released his grip and let the handler arrest the man.

I actually saw the scars on the arm of the man telling the story; it must have been horrific to have experienced that incident, but the strangest thing of all was that sitting at my storyteller's feet was a large male Rottweiler. He bought a Rottweiler years later because he was so impressed with the dog which arrested him, which changed from a ferocious foe one minute to a calm, trained dog the next: even though the dog was badly wounded he never forgot to obey his handler instantly.

THE A.D.R.K.

In the early 1920s the A.D.R.K. (Allgemeiner Deutscher Rottweiler Klub – General German Rottweiler Club) was formed. The A.D.R.K. do much to ensure that the Rottweiler remains correct in mind, heart, health and conformation: a rigid code of conduct for both breeders and owners is maintained, with X-rays for hip dysplasia, hard working trials, tests of suitability for breeding and a great deal more insistence on breeding only from the best than most Kennel Clubs display.

I think it is time the strict A.D.R.K. rules were applied worldwide. If people had to prove good hips by X-ray results, and demonstrate their dogs' bravery, ability to work and good conformation, then we would ensure that the Rottweiler never degenerates into a black and tan

Above: *Rintelna the Bombadier CDEX UDEX, sire of the author's first Rottweiler, Panzer.*

travesty of what once was the best in the world.

It is up to all of us now to make sure that our grandchildren and their children find the Rottweiler as good as they were in days gone by – not 'improved' by exaggerated breed points, but free from painful inherited diseases, sound in mind, retaining that essential inner character of calmness, bravery and ability to work and still looking like real Rottweilers, strong, sound and true.

Let me give you a wonderful quotation by the Countess Aga von Hagen who described the breed in her book published in 1955. "He makes a clear distinction between 'on duty' and 'off duty'. The ferocious guardian becomes a lamb in private life. There is nothing foppish about the Rottweiler. His noble qualities are those of strength, cheerfulness and a warm heart." These lines sum up the traits that typify this breed.

Chapter Two

THE ROTTWEILER PUPPY

Choosing a puppy
Conformation
Checking for problems
Coming home
Crime and punishment
Diet
Socialization
House and garden

CHOOSING A PUPPY AND THE FIRST SIX MONTHS

Having decided that you would like to own a Rottweiler, how do you select the person from whom you will purchase the puppy?

There are weekly dog papers published in most countries which contain advertisements from breeders, and there are also Rottweiler Clubs where information on the breed and lists of breeders can be obtained. The addresses of most clubs can be had from the Kennel Club or the leading official canine body for all breeds. (Some addresses are at the back of this book).

It is essential that you select your breeder wisely, so what do you look for when you visit to discuss the possibility of your buying a puppy?

(a) Check that the breeder is checking you out too: are they asking relevant questions and doing their best to ensure that you are suitable for a Rottweiler?

(b) Are they prepared to show you their official hip dysplasia results of the parents and other related dogs?

(c) Do they have a good after-sales help and advice service should you need guidance from them on rearing and training problems when the pup is growing up?

(d) How do their own dogs behave? Are they obedient, sensible and the kind of dog you want to own?

Above: *A litter of puppies is an irresistible sight, but ask the right questions before buying.*

Below: *An example of a well-designed kennel area, with fire equipment easily to hand.*

(e) The general impression: are the dogs from this kennel well-housed, well-fed, happy and confident? Does the breeder take a real interest in you and your needs and inspire confidence in you? Do you feel that he or she has the ability to help and advise you?

If the answer to all these questions is 'yes', then go ahead and look at the pups (provided, of course, that the breeder is happy with you too). When you look at Rottweiler puppies you cannot always go by the old rule of choosing the one which

Above: *Playtime can be used to form a close relationship with your puppy and to begin to teach it some simple words.*

comes to you, since most Rottweiler pups will rush at you for a fuss – eating your shoelaces and chewing your trouser bottoms!

CONFORMATION

If you are looking for a pup to show later on, select one which conforms as closely as possible

25

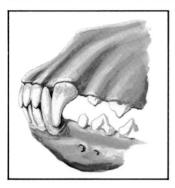

Above: *Check for a scissor bite, where the top teeth fit snugly over the lower ones at the front.*

to the breed standard (see p.100). Look for a broad head with a good stop, neat, high-set ears, dark almond-shaped eyes, and a scissor bite (top teeth fitting neatly over the lower ones at the front).

The body should look neither over-long nor too short, and there should be a big roomy rib cage with strong straight front legs, the feet turning neither in nor out. They should be well knuckled, not spread or flat. The back should be straight, and the part close to the tail (the croup) should not fall away as it does in, for example, the German Shepherd.

The puppy should be viewed from the rear; the hind legs should not be cow hocked. Watch the puppy move about; is it jaunty and true in movement? An experienced dog person will feel for the skeletal structure, ie, the lay of the shoulder, but if you are a novice, look at the pup sideways on; does the neck flow into the body or does it look stuck on as an afterthought?

A pup with a well-laid shoulder will appear to flow nicely

Right: *Look at the puppy from the rear to make sure it does not have cow hocks (when the hind legs bend inwards as shown).*

together, neck with body, and a pup with good shoulders usually has a nicely angulated rear too.

Do not look for over-angulation in Rottweilers, but you do not want back legs which are dead straight, thin and lacking in power. The back end is the 'motor'; it provides the propulsion. If you do not have a good back end you do not have much of a working dog.

Overall, is the pup pleasing to the eye? Remember, if you want a pup to show, you should know your breed standard by heart and perhaps have attended a few shows to 'get your eye in'.

For the person choosing a pup to work, I would pick one with panache that is full of itself. My own preference for a working dog is to pick a slightly longer backed pup, as they seem to

Above: *Check the puppy all over for any signs of lice, which look like grains of sand, and fleas.*

have more ease with jumps and agility later on. I would also like to see if the parents work well too, as I am sure the desire to work is inherited.

The vast majority of people are looking for a companion guard, so they are not interested in breeding, working or showing and can therefore accept minor faults. A pup with a few white hairs on the chest will be just as good a dog to live with as one without, and you probably would not even notice if your pup had a lighter eye than is desirable. I even find that some people actually ask for, and are prepared to await, a long-coated

27

Rottweiler. They are very handsome, but taboo for breeding or showing. You can expect to pay a little less for a dog which is not up to show standard; some breeders only give a pedigree and no registration with a pet puppy. It is a good idea, since it does stop indiscriminate breeding.

However, if you think that you may like to have a litter later on, then please pick a really good pup and pay the correct price. Do not forget that we all want to improve the breed and not see it deteriorate: the Rottweiler is in trouble enough from people breeding from poor stock.

CHECKING FOR PROBLEMS

Check the puppy for fleas, lice or other parasites. Lice look like grains of sand and feel like little scabs. Fleas are hard to see in black coats, but look out for gritty black bits or the fleas themselves. The ears should be clean, with no sign of ear mites (brown, greasy secretions in the ears). Examine the eyes, look for signs of inturning eyelids (a condition called entropion, which causes great distress and usually means surgery later on).

The front dew claws can be left on but the back ones should have been removed.

Look at the puppy's stomach: it

Below: *While you are examining the puppy look inside the ears for ear mites.*

Bottom: *Look for a broad head with a good stop. Ears should be neat and high-set, eyes almond-shaped and dark.*

should be clean and free from rashes or pimples, and there should be no discharge from the genital areas. Male puppies should be gently felt to ensure that two testicles are present; in a very young pup they may not be easy to find! Look at the 'belly button' area; a lump there means a hernia. Some disappear as the pup grows, but some may need surgery. Ask when the pup was wormed, and the name of the product used – your puppy could be afflicted later and you may need to worm again.

Above: *Examine the puppy's stomach to see that there is no genital discharge or hernia.*

COMING HOME

Your breeder should supply you with a diet sheet and some may even give you a supply of the feed to which your pup has been used, in order that it will not get loose motions from a change of diet, home, and the general trauma of the move.

The first night is usually noisy. Give the pup a warm place to sleep with a cardboard box (*not* a stapled one) for a bed, as it is cheap, draughtproof and not dangerous if chewed. Do not go and comfort the pup during the night, or it will howl for you to come again. Do not let the pup

sleep on your bed – it may seem a good idea at eight weeks, but in a year's time 100 lb (45kg) plus of Rottweiler on your bed will give you bad leg cramps.

My personal preference is for a puppy to be reared in the house if it is to achieve its full potential as an adult: just living with you on an every day basis teaches the pup so many things. Without even realizing it, when your puppy is with you all the time you are teaching it the rules of life.

Should you wish to have a kennel and run outside for later on, it must be well constructed and lined, as any projecting edge will be chewed! A wooden floor raised from the ground is best, as it is warmer than concrete, and there should be a strong chew-proof bed. Metal – that is, aluminium angle section – can be used on the edges of the box. Sawdust on the floor is my choice, but you can use newspaper if you wish, though I find it goes soggy and disintegrates easily, making cleaning out a messy business.

The run can be concrete, or a concrete perimeter path with a shingle area inside. You will need to dig out to a depth of about 12 inches (30cm) and fill with shingle; this is easy to clean and disinfect. Some people use paving slabs, but when excrement gets between the cracks it is not very hygenic. Drainage is important; the water must have somewhere to go when you hose out your run, so think of that aspect too.

It is essential that the puppy in the house has access to an outside area for the purpose of toilet training and for playing in the fresh air and sunshine – two vital things. There is nothing like getting a bit of sun on their backs for raising healthy puppies.

It is important that you play with your puppy. There are all kinds of dog toys on the market, or you can make your own from the leg of an old pair of jeans with a knot in it. This makes a lovely tugging toy, which you can use for throwing and playing tug-of-war, as it is strong, cheap and cannot harm your pup. If you can obtain a block of hardwood, this makes a good chew toy, as it

doesn't disintegrate. We found an old hardwood cylinder which was once used as a roller in a machine. It has survived 11 generations of pups and is still going strong.

Never give your puppy an old slipper or shoe, since old shoes look and smell just like new ones, with the inevitable consequences. Never use tennis-sized balls with adult Rottweilers, as these can become lodged at the back of the throat and suffocate your dog – always buy the extra-large solid rubber dog balls, which are much safer. Our adults love to play with old tyres – we roped one to an old apple tree and it is very popular to grab and swing on. They like to play with tyres on the ground too.

When the puppy is sleeping, it must be allowed to relax in peace. The children must be taught that the puppy's bed is sacred, and never to disturb a pup sleeping; then, when the pup

Below: *A tug-of-war can be fun for both you and the puppy. Make sure the puppy 'gives' the object when the game is over.*

has had enough of playing, it knows that its bed is a safe sanctuary.

When visitors come, do not let them encourage your puppy to chew at their clothes; a firm 'No', accompanied by a sharp slap, will stop most pups. It is not a

good idea to let your puppy use you or your visitors as a biting toy. Most men, for some reason, like to play rough wrestling games with puppies. I do not think this is a good idea as, if you let the pup win, it could get the idea that you can be beaten – not a good attitude at all for a pup to adopt – or, if you win all the time, you diminish the pup's self confidence and could even damage it physically. It is much better to play tug-of-war, throwing and fetching games, etc, as these aid training and are just as much fun.

Below: *A block of hardwood, a dog ball, the leg of an old pair of jeans and a bone are safe toys.*

Bottom: *An old tyre can provide hours of great amusement as well as healthy exercise.*

CRIME AND PUNISHMENT

If you need to rebuke a young pup, shake it quite hard by the scruff of the neck and use a very angry voice – just the way the mother would rebuke a pup. If you could see how hard a good mother checks her pups you would not worry about being too tough. Should your puppy decide to retaliate, repeat the rebuke even harder till the pup squeals, then instantly let go and return to normal. The rules are: if you need to punish, it must be the instant the pup is doing the bad deed; it must be strong, accompanied by an angry voice; and forgiveness must be just as swift – never, never nag!

When you feed your puppy, you *must* teach it to allow you to remove the dish or touch it when it is feeding – there is nothing worse than an adult Rottweiler

Below: *Teach your puppy at an early stage that it must allow its dinner bowl to be removed.*

Bottom: *Max gives' his bone. Always ensure adults are present when children are handling dogs.*

which is possessive over food, bones or toys. Start while it is young; give your pup its dish of food, then sometimes put a few extra bits in by hand and other times take the dish, so that your pup accepts your will at all times and learns that your hand coming in may mean that it gets extra goodies. If your pup growls, rebuke it, with a slap or a shake – telling it what a very good puppy it is when it stops growling, and adding a few tasty morsels by hand to the bowl.

The same applies to toys. Teach your pup to 'give' or 'leave' when it has a toy, with much praise when it does and a little game as a special reward. Praise and Punishment are key words,

Above: *The leg of an old pair of jeans, tied in a knot, is a good toy for a tugging game.*

but always be fair and never, ever punish in temper; you will go over the top and that is never a good thing. If you need to punish, make it swift. One hard slap and a really angry voice followed by instant forgiveness is much better than silly little slaps, nagging or, worse, a severe beating.

It should never be necessary to beat any dog severely if it is raised correctly. I very seldom have even to slap my own dogs because they fear my angry voice, and they know that I will punish them if I have to – so usually I do not have to, since they all have respect and love for me. The fear of what I might be able to do is greater than actually knowing my limitations! Beating severely only shows the dog the extent of punishment and may even harden the dog. Rottweilers do not care too much about physical pain, but you can break their hearts easily once they give you all their love and trust. It is better to do things the easy way and gain their love and respect from puppyhood.

You can actually teach your dog to bite you if you punish him by thrashing. Think about it: if the pain is so severe, he will almost *have* to bite you out of self preservation to make you stop. So remember always: one hard slap is better than a beating. Do it from puppyhood and you will end up with a dog on which you only need to use verbal rebukes.

Try always to get into the mind of your dog. Think about life from

Below: *Your dog should wait when the door is opened. Rushing ahead is dangerous.*

the puppy's point of view, bearing in mind that the puppy's mind is simple and not in any way capable of human reasoning; but if you, instead, can 'think like a dog', you will be a little more understanding.

A dog is a pack animal, and it needs its human to be a good 'pack leader'. It should be shown the rules in a simple way: no dog pack leader would allow a member of the pack to cheek him, precede him through a door

or give him any aggravation at all. The offender would be quickly bowled over and bitten hard to remind it of its place.

We ask dogs to live by our laws but we must try to understand a little of their ancestral laws too. Dogs are still possessed of their primitive instincts. For example, if a member of the pack is injured and yelping, the pack will kill it; survival of the fittest is the rule. It sounds harsh to us, but it is a kinder way than leaving an

Above: *The dog is a pack animal and as such still obeys primitive laws of dominance and survival within the group it inhabits.*

injured member to die slowly over several days. Circling to make a bed is on a par with trampling down the grass in the wild. Bone burying is to preserve food and the constant urination of males is to mark territory: it is all part of their inborn heritage.

DIET

Your breeder will have given you a diet sheet which you should try to stick to as far as possible. There are dozens of ways to feed a dog well, but remember it needs to have a well-balanced diet. Shown below is my own simple diet sheet which has been tried and tested over a period of 25 years or so:

First meal: All in one meal, well soaked with puppy milk.
Second meal: All in one meal, soaked with cooked mince, fish or hard-boiled eggs.
Third meal: As first
Fourth meal: As second, but add ½ tsp vitamin and mineral compound
Three months: Three meals daily
Six months: Two meals daily
One year: One meal daily

Don't fall into the trap of overdosing your pup with vitamins – stick to one good vitamin supplement, which must have calcium, phosphorus and Vitamin D in the correct quantities. Do not use several products or you will end up with severe skeletal disorders. Cod liver oil is dangerous – a tiny drop daily is all right, but most people think that if a tiny drop is good, then a jolly good splosh is even better. I have seen the results of jolly good sploshes – puppies with bent legs, in pain all the time. Don't do it!

A growing Rottweiler needs a diet consisting of about half protein and half carbohydrate. Many people use the all-in-one feeds and as they are fairly high in protein you only need to add a little extra protein for a balanced diet if this is what you are feeding. These products are also vitaminized, so to be on the safe side use less of your supplement than is stated on the pack.

If you use milk powder, make sure it is a brand name product, as some pet shops sell calf weaner in plain bags as puppy milk, and this will scour the pup very badly (that is, cause diarrhoea).

Many people worry over the quantity of each meal. I stick to the method my father used with his Bull Terriers – approximately the size of the pup's head per meal – and this works well. With an eight-week old pup on four meals a day, the head is small; then, when the pup is twelve weeks and going on to three meals daily, the head is larger so the meals get larger too. Simple but effective!

Do not forget to leave fresh water available at all times in a heavy bowl. Pups love to pick up water bowls for some reason and the floor gets very wet. However, an earthenware bowl is slippery to pick up, heavy, and not so much fun as a plastic or steel bowl.

Keep your puppy lean, not fat, if you want your adult Rottweiler to be free of hip dysplasia. Young bones should not have to carry excess poundage if they are to grow straight and true, so no choc-drops, pieces of cake or other rubbish! Do not fatten your puppy in order to win puppy classes; it is far better to keep the pup lean and win Open Classes later on with a dog which has good hips. I have been appalled when judging puppy classes to see the waddling puddings in the ring and make a point of telling the owners off after the judging.

Top right: *A large juicy bone will invariably be a favourite toy, guaranteed to keep any dog engrossed for ages.*

Right: *Puppies must not be overfed. Remember that overfeeding and too many vitamins can lead to bad hips and poor health. Puppies must always be kept lean.*

SOCIALIZATION

Socialization is an important aspect of puppy rearing. Take your pup out in the car from day one. *Do not* take him out of the car as he will not have had all his inoculations, but just drive around the block so that the pup does not grow up to be travel sick. Visit friends with the pup and give it as much socialization as possible.

After the pup has had its final inoculations and been blood-tested for parvo virus levels, then the real work can begin. Take the pup to the school to collect the children, visit your local pub or bar with it, and walk a little way down the high street so the pup sees traffic, people and other paraphernalia of modern life. It is not a bad idea at this stage to take out some veterinary and third party insurance – it could save you money later on.

Enrol at your local training class and do about ten minutes in the park daily with the pup off the lead, so that it can meet other dogs. Do not let the pup rampage around too much in play, as they are easily damaged at this age, and do not overdo the exercise; ten minutes is enough at first. It is dangerous to over-exercise a young Rottweiler because they need all their calories to be used in growing rather than in too much exercise and, most important, too much wear and tear on soft, growing bones can cause damage to the skeletal structure. In the garden at home the pup will play and then flop down to sleep. That is good, natural exercise, with the

Below: *A puppy must be socialized so that it will learn not to harass other animals.*

Above: *A well-trained dog and cat can live together in perfect harmony. teach you puppy at once that it is not acceptable behaviour to torment the cat.*

chance to rest when need be.

Many people ask when to use a check chain on the pup. I like to use a light leather puppy collar until the pup is used to the lead and I never use a check chain until the pup is leaning into the collar and is happy enough with the feel of it to pull ahead. There is no rule as every pup is an individual, but generally I do not use a check chain until about six months and then it is essential to use it correctly (see p.55).

If you have another dog or cat in your home when the new pup arrives, you must allow the older dog to growl at the pup if it torments; do not expect the established dog to take to the pup instantly. Pups are a pest to older dogs at first, with their needle teeth and playful ways. Let the older dog chastise the pup when need be while you act as a good referee. Tell the dog that he is still number one and make a great fuss of him too, and you will find that they will become friends.

Your cat will probably feel like leaving home when a pup arrives, so you must let your little Rottweiler know from the first that it must not harry the cat, and in a week there will be peace.

It is not clever to teach your dog to chase cats as there could come a day when your dog chases a cat across the road and is killed; anyway, the cat could be some child's much loved pet!

I hope that you checked all your garden fences for gaps before the puppy arrived – your neighbours will not love you if the puppy gets into their garden and eats their flowers. It is important to keep in with your neighbours when you have a dog; if it is a nuisance to them it is not unknown for a piece of poisoned meat to be flung over the fence. As usual, it is the dog who suffers.

HOUSE AND GARDEN

It is very useful to have some sort of playpen where the puppy can be popped when necessary. We all have days when the phone is ringing, the children are yelling and the pup is being a pest, and it is far better to put the pup in the playpen for an hour than end up getting angry with everyone. At first the pup may yelp to come out, but it is important that you teach it to remain where you wish it to be, so persevere. Obviously, you should not leave the pup in a pen for too long or it will begin to hate the area. Make sure that it has toys and perhaps a few large dog biscuits to chew on, and never take the pup out till it has stopped yelling! Do not give in – your dog must never beat you at anything.

Be careful about shoving young children and puppies unsupervised into the garden just for a bit of peace – my young niece, aged three, was once caught bouncing an eight-week old pup on its head by the back legs! Little children do not realize that they can be very cruel so please, *always* supervise.

Some pups pick up stones, plastic toys and other rubbish, which they swallow. This can cause a blockage, in which case the pup will be listless, off its food and either not passing motions or getting very liquid motions. At any sign of being off-colour you should call your veterinary surgeon; if you know that your pup is a picker-up of such rubbish, tell the vet so that he will know all the facts.

When you leave your puppy for any period, try to look around the room and remove any items which look chewable, for example shoes, children's toys,

Below: *Newspaper makes a warm bed. Change it frequently or it will disintegrate, making a mess.*

etc. Electric flex should have a barricade of some sort so that you don't get a fried puppy. Dangling tea towels are fair game and knobs which stick out just have to be tasted. I once heard of a method for anti-pup chew paste, consisting of chilli peppers, the hottest available, boiled in oil until they formed a paste which could be painted on to areas which get chewed. Mustard is good, too, but some very naughty pups seem to think it adds flavour!

Bitter aloes is another herb which is also said to work well, although I think that it is better to give the pup a distraction. Take a marrow bone, remove the knobby ends with a hacksaw, push out the marrow and push a bit of cooked meat right into the middle of the bone so the pup cannot reach it; they spend hours trying to get it out and ignore the rest of the room.

> So, let us re-cap a little:
> (a) *Don't* have a fat puppy
> (b) *Don't* over-exercise
> (c) *Do* socialize
> (d) When you need to rebuke, use a hard slap or shake accompanied by a very angry tone; a rebuke must be swift, hard and over quickly, with instant forgiveness
> (e) Praise must be lavish – combine fun with firmness

One final word: do not encourage your pup to be aggressive. They guard quite naturally from about 18 months onwards and if you try to 'sharpen up' the pup, you may well end up holding a tiger by the tail. Rottweilers do not need egging on; they do the job of protecting quite naturally.

Below: *Outdoor games in the fresh air and sunshine are the best thing for growing puppies.*

Chapter Three

TRAINING AND BEHAVIOUR

TRAINING PROBLEMS

You should start to train your Rottweiler as soon as you get it – puppy training is a steady ongoing procedure. Begin with house training, ie, where and where not the pup can relieve itself. Leave lots of newspapers by the back door for the pup to use as a toilet, depending on the age of the pup. They cannot usually wait all night until at least 12 weeks. Vigilance is the key word with house training: put the pup out of doors after every meal and watch for signs of sniffing and circling – this means that it needs to 'go'.

Praise like mad for all toilets done outside. Some people manage to make their pups think that the act of going to the toilet at all is bad, thus making their dogs 'secret piddlers': they feel the need to piddle, or worse, only when they cannot be seen by humans – not nice when you find wet patches behind the sofa!

It must be made clear that certain places, ie outside, are good, and inside is bad. The crate system is a good one; using the principle that a dog hates to soil his sleeping place, it is popped into a large wire crate last thing at night and let out in the morning into the garden. You must, of course, accustom the dog to the crate gradually for short periods during the day so that it becomes a comfortable place and not a punishment. Try feeding the pup in the crate so that it associates it with pleasure. Never leave the pup for hours in the crate during the day – a little and often is the rule.

Most puppies will come to a pleasant calling sound as they associate this with the arrival of food. I always yell, 'Puppies come,' when I go to the paddock to feed them. Whatever wonderful game is being played will cease as soon as they hear that call, and they come flying for their food. Thus I have begun to teach them what 'come' means. Sometimes I just go out and call 'Puppies come' when I want to play with them. It has the same effect; they rush up for a romp and a cuddle, and I am establishing a reward for 'coming' – food, play or affection.

BEGINNING TRAINING ROUTINES

When the puppies leave the litter and enter the house to begin the real business of learning, then you, as the owner, have to learn too. Try to do little things each day. For example, even a tiny eight-week-old pup can learn to 'speak'. Wait till just before feed time and show the pup a tasty morsel. It will try to jump up for it, but stare into the pup's eyes and say, quickly and excitedly,

'Speak.' I have had the most amazing results at this age, but it is essential to convey excitement and give the morsel instantly the pup makes a noise. You must do this exercise with no distractions, as a pup cannot concentrate for long. Try to pick a time when nobody is liable to enter the room or move suddenly, as once the pup's eyes leave yours, you have broken the spell. 'Speak' is a handy command, as your dog can use it to convey his needs. Mine will 'speak' to the tap over the sink when thirsty, 'speak' at the door when they need to go to the toilet, or sometimes 'speak' to me, when I have to decipher whether it is 'out', 'water', 'play with me', or 'something's wrong'.

It is useful, too, when you get a caller whom you distrust, to hold the dog by the collar and command 'Speak'. Nobody wants to argue with a Rottweiler under those circumstances and trouble just seems to melt away.

Communication is a good thing between you and your dog, and if it knows 'speak' it can draw your attention to so many things. There is no need to worry that your Rottweiler will bark all day; it is just not in their nature and

Below left: *Rottweilers are highly intelligent dogs and can swiftly acquire the knack of dealing with their needs about the house. Here, 'Max' opens the door.*

Below: *'Max' effects an entry to the kitchen. It is useful to train your dog to 'speak' to be let out, to ask for water and to communicate other needs.*

they use their voice only when the need arises.

ESTABLISHING SUPREMACY

With a tough breed such as this you have to constantly remind it of your supremacy. One way is to teach your pup to 'back' when you open a door, making the pup take a few steps back and not scrabble at the door as soon as you move to open it. Every time you open the door, put your foot against the pup's chest and push it, saying, 'Back.' If the pup ignores you, push it a little more roughly and give your voice an angry edge. The reasons for teaching this simple lesson are:

(a) It shows your dog that you are in charge
(b) It stops your dog rushing into possible danger
(c) When the dog is adult and you open the door to the postman or the paper boy, who may have a hand raised to deliver a letter or paper, your dog is under control just behind you ready to defend you – but in the 'stay' position until you give the next command. If the caller is peaceful and legitimate, you know that your well-trained dog will not rush out and bite him.
(d) Dogs which fight to get out of the door before their owner are a nuisance and, if you live by a busy road, they could easily be

killed. You could also have a bill
for several thousands of pounds
for damages your dog did to the
car – so teach this easy lesson.

The same applies to the car.
The dog must learn to 'stay' until
you say it may enter or leave it –
this is a life-saving lesson. If your
dog leaps from the car on to a
busy road, the consequences
could be awful.

Let us talk about teaching the
'stay'. Little pups can learn to do

Below: *Your dog must learn to
'stay' in the car until you give the
command to leave it. Leaping
from the car on to a busy road
may have fatal consequences.*

Above: *If your dog knows how to
open the door make sure it
knows how to close it as well.*

'baby stays' for a few seconds,
increasing weekly. Adults should
know already what 'stay' means.
Methods are varied, but the
easiest is as follows.

Put your dog on a lead, which
must be long and preferably
leather (see p.60), place the dog
in the 'sit' position and give a
firm command 'Stay',
accompanied by a hand signal
(see illustrations). Take a step
back from your dog, making sure
the lead is slack! The first time
you do it your dog will probably
move, so make a scolding noise
(I use a growly 'Aaargh' sound,
but you can say 'No' if you like)
and put the dog back in the exact
position it was in before. Persist
until the dog stays for five
seconds, then step back to it,
count to three in your head, and
praise the dog effusively. Do not
do too much at first, but do not
give in until you are successful.
Ten minutes is ample.

Why count to three when you
return to your dog? It teaches the
dog to wait until it is released
from the command; you do not
want the dog leaping all over you
when you return to it. I use a

special word which tells my dogs the exercise is over. I say 'OK.' This means the dog is no longer doing the exercise and can relax.

One very important thing is the way in which you say the word 'stay'. It should convey to the dog, 'You have no choice, you *have* to do it.' So many people say 'stay' in the sort of voice that says 'oh, please do it, dear.' It must be a command, not an entreaty.

Do you see how every little step has a reason? For the short daily time you spend teaching your dog civilized behaviour in the first year you will be

Above: *When your dog has learnt to 'stay' step backwards, going a little further each time.*

Below: *Release the dog from the 'stay' position by giving the command to 'come'.*

rewarded with ten or more years with a dog which will be a pleasure and pride to own. When it knows the rules they are there for life.

Once your dog is doing 'stay' on the lead steadily, and clearly knows what you mean, then drop your lead and go further back from it. The next step is to remove the lead and do the exercise. Gradually increase the length of time until your dog will stay for about ten minutes.

Do each exercise step by step; do not be afraid to go back to square one if you need to. In training it is best to progress slowly, and ensure the dog learns each step well. You can eventually go out of sight and know that your dog will stay. One warning; don't do what my husband did. He left his Rottweiler bitch at the 'down stay', became engrossed and forgot her for three hours. She stayed, but he felt terrible! Always release the dog once the exercise is over. Dogs are not robots, so please be fair to them.

Below: *Your dog should learn to 'sit' when he reaches you to complete the exercise.*

'NO!'

You also need a word which tells your puppy that it is doing something bad. 'No' is the most common word, or 'leave' if the puppy is about to chew the carpet or rake out the rubbish bin. Whichever word you use, don't keep changing it; make it easy for a tiny mind to understand. Should your pup ignore the word, either you are being verbally too soft, or you have a pretty dominant pup. Try a second command in a much fiercer tone. If the pup ignores you again, either go up and give it a hard shake by the scruff of the neck, accompanied by an even stronger 'no' or throw an object at the pup. Some Rottweiler pups will try to bite you when corrected, so you must win. Never let a pup get away with aggression towards you; you must give it a very hard slap to establish your authority. Don't forget to make friends again the minute the pup submits. Your total attitude should convey your supremacy to the pup.

It is noticeable how people with natural authority with dogs seldom need to use force.

Somehow the dog just knows that there is a person with whom they will never get away with nonsense. Try to cultivate this frame of mind and it works wonders. Your tone of voice is of prime importance: you must be able to sound totally venomous and, seconds later, you may need to use a voice absolutely dripping with honey. A simple 'Good dog' is not always enough – make your praise lavish and your punishing voice frightening.

I have a magic word: it is 'Right'. This means 'You have gone too far and I am now really angry'. It must be rapped out in a sharp, threatening way – it terrifies my dogs and even works on those I work with which have been trained in other languages. If said in the correct way the word conveys such menace that the message gets through.

MORE COMMANDS

It is also necessary to teach your dog to lie flat. You should use a command and hand signal. Point to the floor, say a firm, decisive 'Down', push the pup behind the shoulders and down he goes. You can also pull out the front legs from a sitting position, or roll him over with a push on the shoulder sideways on. There are harsher methods for older dogs, but you should not need to use them on a pup. Do a little exercise for a few minutes in this command, say five or six times a day, with lots of praise, and within a week your pup will know what 'down' means.

Then you can do 'down stay' for ten seconds, slowly building up to ten minutes. Never forget that pups lack concentration, so do not push on too quickly, and always have a little game after training as a reward.

At about three to four months your pup will start to become more independent and will sometimes refuse to come. Always use the dog's name, for example, 'Rex, come', not just 'Rex', which tells it its name but not what to do. If there is no response, your next move is to pick up an object (a plastic bowl is good) and toss it hard so that it hits the pup. The impact should be accompanied by 'Rex, come', followed instantly by 'Good dog' when it takes a step towards you and more praise as it continues to come. The pup soon learns that no matter where it is you can

Below: *'Down stay', where the dog lies down rather than sitting, is another useful command.*

make something bad happen to it if it chooses to disobey.

With an older dog, you can throw something harder. A heavy check chain is good, but it must be thrown strongly enough to hurt or the exercise is useless.

Never, never hit a dog when it comes, no matter how angry you are, or you will finish with a dog which is afraid to come to you.

There are people who do not believe in being hard on a dog. That's fine, but such people should never buy a Rottweiler as the breed needs a very firm hand, sometimes on the rump, pretty sharply!

Jumping up is another thing which the pup needs to know about. You need to start teaching the words 'off' or 'get off' from day one. Little muddy paw prints on the fridge door, or your

Above: *Jumping up on command is acceptable; uncontrolled, however, it can be a menace.*

friend's best suit, are not endearing things, so teach your pup by using the word accompanied by a tug on the puppy collar: you should also ask all visitors to help you by using the same word. Don't ever say, 'Oh, it's OK for you to jump up on Fred as he is wearing old jeans, but you can't jump on Auntie Maud,' as that is too confusing for it. The pup either can jump up or it cannot.

It is not a good idea to let pups go up and down stairs as it has a bad effect on bone structure and could be damaging, so when little Rex puts his paws on the stairs say 'Get off.'

RETRIVING

Teething is a time when a puppy's gums hurt and it needs to chew hard objects, so give it suitable things. Playing tug-of-war with the leg of an old pair of jeans is a good game and helps to pull out the baby teeth. There is a school of thought which says that such games make teeth go undershot but, speaking from experience, I have not found it to be so. It's good fun, a lovely reward game and you can start your retrieve this way too.

Play tug-of-war, then throw the cloth into a corner; your pup will rush to get it and bring it back for another game. If the pup runs off with the cloth, put yourself in a position in the room where you can intercept the pup next time you throw it and take the cloth away. Soon the dog will realize that by bringing the cloth to you the game gets even better. Don't forget to give the command 'Fetch' when you throw the cloth, and within weeks your pup will know another word.

When you give the cloth to the pup, say 'Hold it'. When the pup takes it, praise highly. If you do this every time you give the pup a toy, it will soon know the words 'hold it' – another step on your way to a good retriever. One tip – always finish a retrieve game while the pup is still keen to do it. Never go on until the pup gets fed up, or you will undo all your good work. If you use a retrieve article, such as a dumb-bell, two retrieves are enough, then put the dumb-bell in a place where the pup can see it, but cannot reach it. You can then talk to the pup about it from time to time, saying things like 'There's your lovely 'fetch' ', and making the pup really want the article.

COMMUNICATION

Talking to your dog is very necessary; not just commands, but normal chat. It is probably seen to be a sign of madness by some people, but then they do not get as much enjoyment and co-operation from their dogs as those who do talk to them. It is important to have a good relationship with your dog – you must understand each other's needs and ways, and talking to the dog is companionable and sociable. You would be surprised

Below: *Early games with your puppy can lead quite easily to training for the retrieve. Good fun for you and your dog.*

Above: *Don't be dissuaded from introducing your dog to other animals. It is always of help.*

at how many words a dog can pick out of a sentence and understand, especially if you speak in a voice which is not a dull monotone. Most dogs know the words 'walk', 'going out' and 'do you want'; they soon learn 'dinner' or 'water' from just listening and association of ideas.

You will notice how quickly a dog learns how certain actions performed by the human in its life affect it. Going to the cupboard where the dog food is kept at certain times means that dinner is coming, putting on certain clothes means that it might be time for a walk, or other clothes mean that it is definitely not time for a walk.

Some Rottweilers have a great sense of humour and will use their mind in a quite uncanny way. For example, a friend of

mine is a cab driver and when he is going to work he always puts on a particular pair of shoes. His Rottweiler noticed this and, sneakily, began to hide just one of the shoes every day, resulting in a frantic half hour search to find the shoe: the dog did not like his owner leaving him, and tried in his simple way to stop it happening. Some scientists do not believe that a dog is capable of such simple reasoning power, but there is a wealth of difference between a laboratory animal and a socialized trained dog, which is taught to use its mind.

As I have said before, if you keep a Rottweiler outside in a kennel it will never develop its full potential as a house pet does. Certainly it is hard work to teach a pup, but look at the rewards – and anyway, it should be good fun too. Training should be enjoyable for you and the dog. There is nothing like the feeling of elation you get when the dog finally understands and performs the action want.

CHECKING AGGRESSION

For those of you who already have a Rottweiler, fully grown and perhaps giving you some trouble, here are some of the main problems and a few tips on how to deal with them.

Aggression over food should, of course, have been dealt with in babyhood, but if it wasn't, your dog may be growling over food, bones or possessions. It is always better not to have a stand-up fight with a fully grown Rottweiler unless you are sure you can win! Therefore, you have to beat it with craftiness.

Tie a piece of string round the food bowl with a long length to your hand, get an empty washing-up-liquid bottle and fill it with very cold water (or, in the case of very bad dogs, you can use a small saucepan full of icy water). Put down the bowl and, when the dog begins to eat, say 'Leave'. The dog will not obey you and may growl ominously. Say again, in a very firm voice, 'Rex, leave,' and give the dog a squirt in the face from the bottle, or a good slosh from the saucepan of water. This will usually cause the dog to stop eating in surprise. Then, with a quick tug, pull the bowl to you and pick it up, at the same time praising the dog for 'leaving'. Let the dog then see you drop a few tasty morsels into the bowl and give it back.

This will prove to your dog that you can compel it to 'leave' and also that you sometimes only want the bowl to add a little extra. You can see now why you need to sort out this problem in puppyhood; a fully grown adult who has not learned early that his owner is omnipotent is a very difficult problem.

You *must* win all the time. Take the trouble to think of solutions yourself; you have a superior brain to your dog (at least I hope so), so always be prepared to find sneaky ways to combat your dog's power.

Above: *If you see an obviously aggressive dog approaching do not tense up, as this will tell your dog that you are anxious. Walk on in a relaxed manner.*

Left: *A bone will be a prized possession, but train your dog to allow you to approach and take away its food.*

Aggression with other dogs is another problem, usually found in males rather than females, and although I have seen some aggressive Rottweiler bitches, they are much rarer. It is very hard work to stop adult males from being aggressive if they were not stopped the very first time they showed such tendencies. The best way is to use a check chain.

If you see trouble brewing, for example the approach of a dog not on a lead, *do not* tense up and tighten your lead, as this tells your dog that you are anxious and it will react immediately. Instead, tell your dog to 'leave it' and continue to walk on in a relaxed manner, but be ready. When the other dog is

about 20ft (6m) away and your dog lunges at it, let the weight of your dog going forward meet suddenly with your weight going back (which is the purpose of the loose lead – if the lead is tight you cannot do this). A check chain used in this manner gives the dog a shock and it should be accompanied by a tirade of abuse from you. You *must* be prepared to be hard on your dog for unwarranted aggression.

If your dog knows the words 'down stay', another method is to put your dog in this position upon the approach of a loose dog, and carry in your pocket a spare heavy check chain which you can throw at the other dog if it approaches too closely. This may well enrage the dog's owner, but if he or she cannot keep the dog under control, it is better for you to keep it away than for it to be eaten by your Rottweiler.

You can see now why you need a strong personality to own a

Above: *Leave the check chain loose so that when the dog rushes forward the momentum will serve to create a hard jerk of the chain on the dog's neck.*

Above: *When the dog drops back to the normal walking position offer it plenty of praise and continue walking. Never let aggression pass unchecked.*

Rottweiler, but if you train it correctly from puppyhood these problems will not arise.

As a last resort, you can have your male dog castrated. Some people think this is cruel, but look at it logically. Your average run-of-the-mill Rottweiler male is not likely to be used at stud (nor should it be unless it is an outstanding specimen with an HD-Free Certificate). I know you all think that your dog is the most beautiful Rottweiler in the world, but there is an old saying that goes 'There is only one perfect dog in all the world and every owner has it', and it is very true.

The sex drive is only a nuisance to the average male dog: it is a misguided idea that it will help the dog to mate it once. Since you cannot keep up a supply of females, it is kinder for the dog never to be used. Castration is also sometimes kinder from the point of view that it often stops a great deal of sexually related aggression. You must remember, though, that you should never castrate a dog until it has all its male hormones, ie at about 18 months, or it will stay puppylike. Castration after it has all its male hormones will not make it soppy; the dog's character remains the same, except that it has less desire to fight. You must cut down on the dog's food though, as they have a tendency to put on weight.

Above: *It is vital to keep your dog under control at the vet's. Begin training at puppyhood.*

AGGRESSION TOWARDS PEOPLE

There is another kind of problem which causes a great deal of worry, and this is aggression towards the vet if the dog has to be treated for ailments. This should never be allowed: your vet's hands are his livelihood and many vets do not like to treat our breed because of the few 'wrong 'uns' that try to eat the vet and wreck the surgery. A Rottweiler which is under control and has respect for its owner should be good in all circumstances. However, if you did not teach your dog properly and do not have it under control, how do you deal with the problem of a 'vet hater'? Tranquillizers help, but they need to be given well before the visit; you, the owner, should hold the dog's head and, if necessary, tape the dog's muzzle so that it cannot bite; you should also be ready to give the dog a hard thump if it plays up. Whatever you do, do not ever let your dog bite the vet!

Aggression upon the approach of a stranger is a problem which can be very serious. This has to be stopped or the dog's life may be forfeit. It is not brave or protective – in fact, it is generally the opposite; it is caused by fear or nervous aggression. I do not mean the dog which barks when a stranger knocks at the door, but the dog which hackles up and roars at passers-by in the street when out with its owner. Some people think that this is clever, and that the dog is looking after them. Nothing is further from the truth, as most dogs which do this lack self-confidence and would back off if real trouble came along. Again, this is caused usually by a lack of socialization when the dog was young or, in some cases, it is an inherited tendency. Such dogs must *never* be bred from and, if the dog is truly nervous, it is sometimes kinder to have it put down. Personally, I believe that a nervous Rottweiler is a liability and no pleasure to own. It is also potentially dangerous.

However, if the dog was never socialized, then the behaviour is probably not inherited. It is caused by human error and hard, patient work can improve the dog dramatically. You must take the dog to places where it will see people, traffic, and other everyday sights; sometimes just sitting on a park bench with the dog beside you helps. Training

classes help too.

Dogs which lunge at people must be severely chastised – use the method I described earlier for aggression towards other dogs. You can give the dog a very hard slap for this too; in fact, you cannot be hard enough for this behaviour. Bearing in mind that your dog's life is on the line if it bites people, it sometimes pays to get very tough!

Do not forget, however, that most Rottweilers never need such treatment if raised in the correct manner. I only advocate being tough when the dog really needs it.

There are some owners who become afraid of their own dog. This is a grave problem, since the dog will know this from the scent given out and, if you are really afraid of a dog, it will react to this fear scent and become really dominant. I feel that this is one circumstance where it is sometimes better to part with the dog unless you can get skilled help, both to conquer your fear and to teach the dog properly.

Below: *Aggression may be a sign of lack of socialization. Take your dog out and about to accustom it to people and traffic. In this way it will become a safe and trusted companion for all the family.*

Yet another reason to get your
dog under control while it is
young!

DEALING WITH STEALING

Stealing is something I am often
asked about: stealing food from
worktops, dirty washing from
bathrooms, clean washing from
the line, etc. Stealing is not seen
to be a crime by a dog. The
desirable object is within reach
and there is no dog law which
says 'thou shalt not steal'. It is,
however, a crime in human eyes,
so the dog has to learn this. How
do you stop this act? We have a
law in our house: the floor is the
'dog shelf' and if any item is left
on it then it is our fault if it is
taken. This also helps to train the
family not to leave a trail of dirty
socks around the floor, to pick up
toys, etc, so it is a good rule in
most homes. However, stealing
from high places can be stopped
by leaving booby traps.

I once had a dog called
Gamegards Fire & Rain (Condor)
who, through his film work, had
been trained to open cupboard
doors. The refrigerator had a
door which he could easily open
and often when I was outside he
would open it and steal the
cheese. The problem was not just
the theft of the cheese; since no-
one was there to tell him to 'shut
the door' he left it open. This
meant the other house dogs
could raid the rest of the
contents! My solution was a
mouse trap, set with a lump of
cheese. I left it at the front of the
fridge and went outside, but I hid
in a position where I could see
the consequences. Sure enough,
the clever old lad opened the
door and went to take the
cheese. What a shock he got
when the trap went off and the
cheese bit back! It worked well,
but I had to leave the trap set for
a few more days just in case he
tried again. Afterwards, every
time he saw a mouse trap he
would growl at it.
You can leave booby traps of

meat covered with mustard, or
alternatively create a booby trap
from a pile of empty beer cans on
a bit of cardboard. Put some
pebbles in each can and leave
the food on a string from the
board holding the cans. When
the dog takes the food the whole
lot comes down on its head –

quite effective. Use your imagination and be inventive. Do not just accept that your dog steals, but think of ways to stop it. Those are some ideas; maybe you can think of better ones.

Washing on the line is a very tempting thing to a young, playful dog, so either put your

Above: *Care should be taken to keep doors closed and 'chewables' out of reach of inquisitive Rottweilers!*

line too high for it to reach, or put it in a place the dog cannot get to. Use plain common sense.

Above: *This is the incorrect way to loop a check chain. It will not loosen when the dog ceases to put pressure upon it so improved behaviour will not be rewarded.*

Below: *The correct way to loop a check chain. It will loosen as soon as the dog ceases to strain against it. Note that the dog must be on your left hand side.*

ADVANCED TRAINING

Now on to more formal training. You need to learn to use a check chain in the correct manner. Use a very strong check chain, and a

4ft (122cm) long lead made of bridle leather and riveted, with a trigger clip. Look at the photographs of the right and wrong way to put on a check chain; it is essential that the chain is on the dog properly, or it

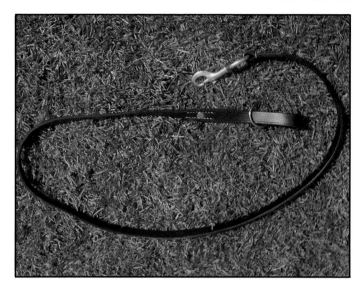

Above: *Choose a strong leash of bridle leather; sewn, riveted and fitted with a trigger clip.*

will not slacken when the pressure is off. The dog, for training purposes, is always on your left hand side because, in competition work, this is always the way it is done.

Your dog should walk at heel with its head about level with your knee or upper thigh, depending on its height. The lead must be loose, as shown in the photograph, and the chain should lie comfortably but very loosely on the neck. When the dog goes to rush ahead or to the side, give a hard, quick, tug on the lead, which will cause the chain suddenly to go tight. It must be almost a snapping motion, as your weight going back meets the dog's weight going forward. Don't just use your wrists or arms – get your shoulders behind the force, too. This action of the loose lead snapping tight will give the dog a shock and you should use the command 'Rex, heel', not forgetting to praise really highly when the dog is back in the correct position.

It is all a matter of good timing – tugging too late when the dog has already taken up the slack in the lead is of no use at all; neither is constantly sawing at the dog's neck with silly little tugs. One good check will show the dog that it is really not worth while to pull on the lead and it will get to love the praise you give it when it does well. (See p.55.)

If you have the opposite problem of the dog hanging back behind you, then go back to a collar and use great encouragement. Keep up a steady stream of chat, such as 'Come on, Rex, what a good little Rex, let's go see what's up here, come Rex', even crouch down and encourage the dog forward. Anything which brings the dog forward in the way of inducement is good. Never, never use force. On a lagging dog it makes the situation worse; you need to build up the dog's confidence, not crush it.

Once the dog has the hang of walking to heel properly, then do a few 'sits'. Walk off, after saying to your dog first, 'Rex, heel', then after a few paces say 'Sit' and press your hand down on the dog's rump, pushing it into the

sitting position. Most dogs, by this time, will know the word 'sit', but you want your dog to sit quickly on the first command when you stop. If you are training for the show ring, when you stop tell your dog to 'stand stay' and spend a few seconds practising with the dog to adopt a good 'stand'; you may use a titbit for this. Some people gently put a foot under the dog's belly to get the idea into the dog's head, but I stress gently. Make the 'stand' command a bit long-drawn-out – 'Staaaand' – and do not use a harsh voice; this word must be encouraging rather than disciplining.

If you are too hard with this exercise the dog will stand like a pile of rice pudding, whereas you want an alert, attentive stand. If you want to enter your dog in shows later, always tell your dog to 'stand' for a titbit from puppyhood instead of the usual method of 'sit'. Once a dog has learned to sit for a reward of this kind it is very difficult to persuade it to stand – the bottom hits the ground all the time and it can be very frustrating for you and the dog.

Above: *When you are training for shows teach your dog to adopt a good 'stand' for the judge.*

When you are out in an open space, for example the park or fields, spend a few minutes doing some 'sit stay' and 'down stay' exercises and recalls before you let your dog run about freely. It takes a very little time and the run afterwards is an excellent reward. One potentially life-saving exercise is to be able to drop your dog into the 'down' position wherever it is.

To teach this exercise, the dog must, of course, know the word 'down' already. Leave him in the 'sit stay' position and walk away about 20 paces, turn and face him, count to five in your head and then call him. When the dog is about a quarter of the way towards you, say, 'Rex, down,' and take a step or two towards him with your arm pointing to the ground. Do it in an urgent manner – pretend there is a bus about to run the dog over if it continues to come. This will give your voice impact, and cause the dog to check its recall. You may

need to repeat the command or even take a few steps closer. When the dog goes down, go up to it and praise very highly. A word of warning: don't do this exercise too much or it will slow down your recall. Just do it occasionally, until in the end when the dog hears 'Rex, down' it will drop like a stone. It is a very worthwhile exercise.

SUMMING UP

One fault I notice with many would-be trainers is that of nagging when the dog is free and out at exercise. Do try not to do this, or your dog will quickly become bored and soon will ignore your commands because it incessantly hears 'Rex come' 'Rex leave', etc. Call your dog when necessary, of course, but do not keep calling. Let your dog have some peace to sniff and enjoy its walk, but keep an eye open all the time for hazards such as an obviously aggressive dog, farm animals, or even perhaps the sight in the distance of a person wearing a floppy macintosh which, to a young inexperienced dog, might look

Above: *When on a walk allow your dog to enjoy its exercise and do not give commands unnecessarily.*

threatening enough for it to want to bark. Get to know your dog's mind, be one step ahead.

You must be confident that you can control your dog at all times, and of course if you did your homework you will be.

So let us re-cap: *Do* be positive, confident, firm, fun and determined; *Do not* nag, dither, or lose your temper.

Learn how to use your voice clearly so that it conveys the correct message to your dog. Dull monotones are out. Use feeling in the voice – aim for venom and honey!

Enjoy your training, enjoy your dog, and *always win*. If you need help from a more experienced trainer, ask for it, and never be afraid to make haste slowly or go back a step. Never encourage your dog to be aggressive.

Chapter Four

HEALTH PROBLEMS

Hip displaysia
Osteochondrosis
Cruciate ligament
Contagious diseases
Eye problems
Skin problems
Enzyme deficiency
Bloat
Inoculations

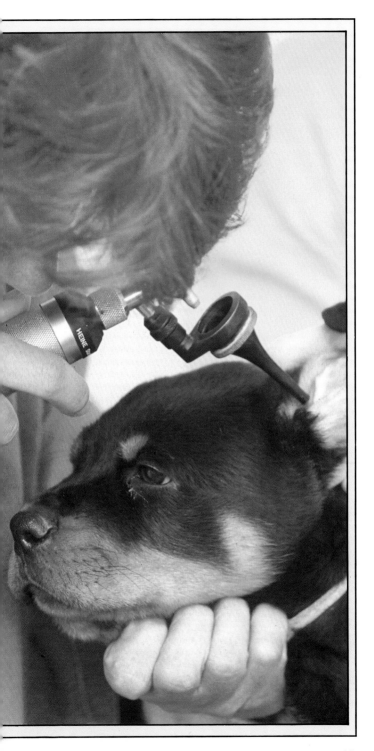

HIP DYSPLASIA

Hip dysplasia (HD) is one of the biggest problems to beset Rottweilers. It is a malformation of the ball and socket joint of the hip – sometimes the cup or, to give it its correct name, the acetabulum, is too shallow, or the ball or femoral head may be misshapen, and this will cause a great deal of pain and arthritis in later life. This distressing condition is thought to be 40 per cent inherited, hence my constant urging for all breeding animals to be hip scored through the hip scheme for the relevant country; only by X-ray can you tell what the hips are like, as you cannot see by the dog's movement unless it is a very bad case. For control schemes, X-rays are done under general anaesthetic at one year. Under the hip scoring scheme, the minimum score for each hip is 0 and the maximun 53; the lower the score, the less the degree of hip dysplasia. The range is thus 0–106 for both hips. A total score of 0–4 (with not more than 3 for one hip) is acceptable, while a score of 5–8 (with not more than 6 for one hip) would indicate that the dog can breed, but its mate must have a lower score. A score of over 8 is a fail.

In the United States a control scheme is run by the Orthopedic Foundation for Animals (O.F.A.). This organization checks a dog's X-rays and pronounces it afflicted or not afflicted. If HD-free, the animal is given an O.F.A. registration number.

HD is a condition that can be controlled by selective breeding

Below: *An X-ray of the hips of a dog with dysplaysia. Note misshapen joint. Selective breeding could help stop this.*

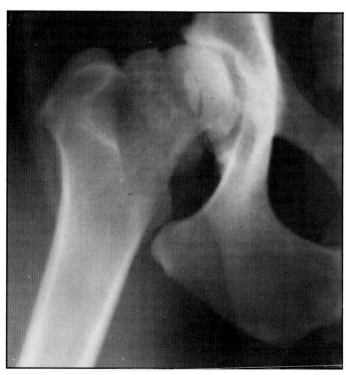

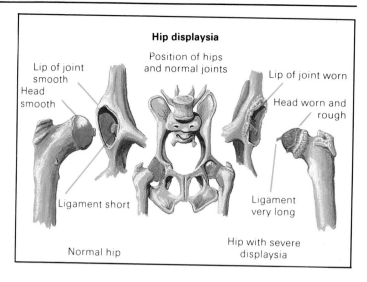

Hip displaysia

Position of hips and normal joints

Lip of joint smooth
Head smooth

Lip of joint worn
Head worn and rough

Ligament short

Ligament very long

Normal hip

Hip with severe displaysia

and careful rearing, so please do not breed from un-X-rayed Rottweilers and do not buy a pup unless you can see the official hip scores.

If you are unlucky enough to own an affected dog, there are surgical procedures which can help. The femoral head can be removed or, in some cases, the pectinious muscle can be cut, which causes the joint to pull apart, alleviating some pain. However this method is not 100 per cent effective, and there are now other operations that are more successful.

OSTEOCHONDROSIS

This is another orthopaedic condition, the cause of which is at present not known. It can affect the shoulder, elbow, hock or stifle joints during the growing period. Bits of cartilage grow and sometimes flake off into the joint, causing a lot of pain and usually necessitating surgery to remove the cartilage pieces.

Any lameness during puppyhood should be investigated by your vet, and rest is essential to minimize the damage. I have had five cases during the last few years, all from different litters, and in four cases

Above: *Shown from below, with legs pushed back: a normal hip compared with one with HD.*

the owners of the puppies had cars with high backs, so there may be a case for making a connection between jumping in and out of high places and osteochondrosis.

CRUCIATE LIGAMENT

This is the cross ligament which runs through the stifle joint (equivalent to our knee), and it can snap or stretch. The dog will carry its leg in a very peculiar manner with the toe pointing to the ground. This, too, needs surgery and fairly quickly, before secondary changes make the damage worse. The dog needs very careful nursing afterwards, being taken on a lead to relieve itself and allowed no other exercise until the leg is strong again. There do seem to be some bloodlines in which this condition occurs more often; my own theory is that it seems to happen more often with the short coupled, very tightly-knit dogs with little hind angulation.

I have only had two cases in 25 years: one in my very first

Rottweiler who, at the age of nine, was hit sideways on by another Rottweiler running really fast. There was a crash of bodies and my dog was lamed; he was operated on and made a full recovery. The second case was a female, aged eight, who jumped a ditch and landed badly. She too had snapped a cruciate, but, after surgery, made a full recovery.

CONTAGIOUS DISEASES

Leptospirosis, hardpad, distemper, hepatitis and parvo virus are the big five killer diseases, with parvo virus the most virulent to our breed. It is essential that all dogs be inoculated at 12 weeks, and boosted annually.

Sickness, diarrhoea (with a never-to-be-forgotten smell) and listlessness should be treated immediately by your vet if the dog has any chance of survival: this is parvo virus. You cannot imagine how quickly a healthy puppy could be transformed into a dehydrated dying skeleton in two or three days: please, never underestimate the value of inoculations for this dreaded disease.

EYE PROBLEMS

Entropion, or inturning eyelids, is usually found in dogs with deepset eyes and with too much loose skin on the head. It causes

pain and may even ulcerate the eye, so consult your vet and have the eye operated on. Do not ignore it, as it will not go away on its own. It is an inherited condition, so do not breed from affected animals.

Conjunctivitis is an infection which causes yellow runny eyes. Your vet will give you an antibiotic ointment which will soon clear it up.

EAR MITES

Brownish secretions in the ear usually mean ear mites. They itch badly, especially when the dog is hot. Do not put just any ear powder in the ear, but get the correct medication from your vet and use it diligently. Check your cats, too, as they get ear mites and will re-infect your dog.

SKIN PROBLEMS

Eczema can be flea-induced and the dog will bite at the base of the tail, causing great raw weeping patches. First get rid of the fleas using a special spray on your carpets, pet bed, etc. Fleas like to live and breed in such places and only hop on the dog to feed. Bath your dog in a good anti-flea shampoo, then paint the eczema with gentian violet – it

Below: *Entropion (inturning) eyelids can cause great distress and may need surgery.*

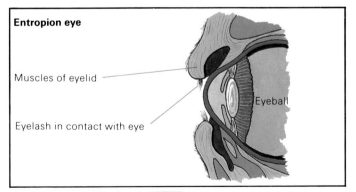

Entropion eye

Muscles of eyelid

Eyeball

Eyelash in contact with eye

tastes horrible, stings a lot, stops the itch and dries up the wet patches. Sometimes play bites on the face will flare up into eczema – use gentian violet again, or get a proprietory cream from the vet.

Mange is another case for the vet. A skin scraping may be taken to ascertain whether it is sarcoptic or follicular mange; both need baths and very careful treatment. It is fairly rare in Rottweilers. An old cure is sump (crankcase) oil and sulphur: empty the used oil from the car sump (crankcase), mix it with yellow flowers of sulphur powder and cover all affected areas well beyond the actual baldness. Keep the dog in a place where it cannot rub on furniture or ruin your decor, as it is very messy. Do it daily for three weeks and it will work like magic. You must always consult your vet as well to be on the safe side.

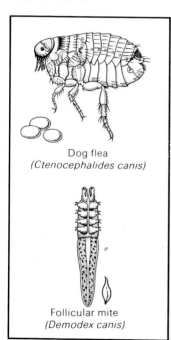

Dog flea
(Ctenocephalides canis)

Follicular mite
(Demodex canis)

Above: *Two types of external parasites with their eggs. Too small to be seen, their effects on a dog can be obvious.*

Below: *Allergic reactions can cause itchy paws. Dogs must be stopped from gnawing them.*

FEET

Some Rottweilers get itchy feet, when they bite and chew until the pads are raw. I think that my own dogs are allergic to some carpet-cleaning powders. I have cured this with a product called Bitter Apple, which stops them chewing immediately.

ENZYME DEFICIENCY

Some Rottweilers do not produce enough enzymes from the pancreas, in which case they fail to body up, have loose motions and are not able to digest fat. If your dog has these symptoms take a sample of faeces to your vet for analysis; the condition can be controlled by adding a pancreatic extract to the diet.

CANCER

This is a condition which sometimes strikes the breed. When it is diagnosed my solution is to give the dog a good end, before it becomes racked with pain. Treatment, in my experience, is seldom successful and I cannot bear to have a dog die slowly and painfully. It is kinder to let the dog quietly go to sleep in your arms with a little help from the vet's needle.

BLOAT

Overfeeding, especially with dry foods, can cause the stomach to swell, twist and kill the dog. A good tip, if your dog is blown up, is to give a walnut-sized knob of common washing soda; if the dog is sick within a few minutes then it is not bloat, as they cannot be sick with true bloat. If the dog is not sick, then get it to the vet *fast*. The remedy is surgical, and seconds are vital if the life of the dog is to be saved.

Below: *Don't risk your pet's life by neglecting vital inoculations. Rottweilers are prone to parvo virus, which can be fatal.*

INOCULATIONS

Rottweilers are very prone to parvo virus (see p.68), so please be sure that your inoculations are kept up-to-date. I give my puppies a parvo inoculation at six weeks just in case any members of the litter have lost their maternal immunity, then at 12 weeks they get the Big Five – distemper, hardpad, leptospirosis, hepatitis and parvo inoculations. Four weeks later they get the second course, then two weeks after that I have the pups blood tested by a vet to be sure that the parvo levels are high enough before taking them out and exposing them to possible infection. It has been

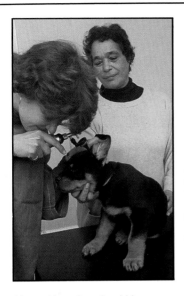

Above: *Your dog should become used to being handled by a vet. Never, ever allow aggression.*

dissuade you, but you should insist. It is a very simple procedure, and not painful. In the first year it is advisable to get a six-month parvo shot, and then a booster for the Big Five diseases every year. Your vet should be able to send you a reminder annually and it is a life-saving procedure which costs little compared with losing your pet.

In the USA, rabies inoculations are required by every state. Pups can be given an inoculation at three months which will provide protection for one year. After the second shot at 15 months boosters will be required every three years.

GENERAL

Basically, the Rottweiler is a fairly healthy breed, but remember that prevention is better than cure: check your dog for parasites, use common sense when out at exercise. Don't fatten puppies, keep them lean, feed them well, but don't over-feed. Keep your eyes open and know your dog well, for a slight change in behaviour could mean that the dog is in pain. Make friends with your vet and be sure your dog does too. You may not need to see the vet often, but when you do be fair to him, telling him all the symptoms clearly, and never call for night visits unless it is a real emergency.

known for pups to have had several parvo shots and still have no immunity, so a blood test is the only way to be sure. Some puppies carry such high levels of maternal immunity (passed on by the mother through the colostrum – first day's milk) that this nullifies the inoculation. When the maternal immunity in the pup wears off it is totally unprotected, even though it has had the shots. Your vet may try to

---

Checklist for health

(a) Feed well, but don't indulge the dog until it gets fat
(b) Don't give 'sweeties'. If you use a titbit for training, hard-bake some little bits of liver, the most popular treat of all
(c) Exercise mind as well as body
(d) Keep all inoculations up to date
(e) Never ignore symptoms of illness
(f) If you get a problem, consult your breeder or vet

(g) Keep an eye open at all times for parasites; fleas, lice and worms. Deal with them immediately.
(h) Watch that claws don't grow too long

Maintaining any dog is a matter of common sense and a little know how: I hope that you already possess the common sense and that I have given you, in this small table, at least a little know how.

Chapter Five

BREEDING THE ROTTWEILER

Choosing a bitch
Choosing a stud
Mating
Whelping
The first weeks

CHOOSING A BITCH

If everyone bred a litter 'because it is good for the bitch', we should all be knee-deep in puppies.

There are several reasons to breed a bitch: if she is a really good specimen of the breed, if she has a perfect temperament and if she X-rayed well under the official scheme. However, you should only breed your bitch if you have the time to give to the pups, the money to raise them well and the space to keep them. They may not all be sold until three or four months old and, at that age, they eat a lot and need inoculations, attention and socialization.

You must be in a position to take back any of your pups if they need to be re-homed. You are responsible for bringing that dog into the world so you must be prepared to help it if necessary. You should also be able to advise your puppy buyers on all aspects of rearing and training, and be at the end of the telephone when they need help.

Many people breed a litter for the money but, if the job is done properly, there is not much profit in it. Most caring breeders like

Below: *Sire with puppies aged seven weeks. Now is the time when socialization should begin in earnest; helped by dad's fine example!*

myself have to work to pay for the cost of keeping their dogs – in my case it is my film and television work with dogs which pays for their keep, one other breeder is a night nurse and yet another works in a garage as a petrol pump attendant, so you can see it is not the way to a fortune!

Whelping kennels have to be lined with good insulating material so that the kennel is draught-proof, and there must be a heater over the whelping box. In very cold weather you may need an extra heater, as newly born pups soon get chilled and will die very quickly; this is all expensive.

However, let us start at the beginning – you have a good quality well-bred bitch, she has a good character, and has X-rayed well. You realize the responsibilities of breeding and are prepared to keep the pups over a period of time if need be, and to vet prospective owners carefully. You have learned something of breed requirements so that you can help and advise the new owners.

Above: *A view of whelping kennels. Note how clean and tidy they are kept. Each bitch has her own kennel for privacy. An interior is shown on p.78.*

CHOOSING A STUD

How to find the best male dog for your bitch? If you already own a male there is the temptation to use him or the dog of a friend nearby. My advice is don't: it is rare that your own dog or a neighbour's dog will suit your bitch in terms of conformation, blood line or anything else. Attend a few shows months before you intend to mate your bitch, get your eye in, and learn correct type. Visit well-known reputable breeders, too, look at their stud dogs and take your pedigree to compare. Know your own bitch's failings and virtues and choose wisely: it is very important that the stud dog has a good hip score, too, and ask about his parents' and grandparents' scores, as the better the background the better

the chance of good hips. Make sure that the stud dog has a good character. If you cannot handle the dog suspect the worst, as many people try to mask a nasty temperament by making excuses. Beware of this, as a dog with good character should be able to be touched.

It is a wise idea to have a vaginal swab done by your vet a few weeks before your bitch is due in season. It is amazing how many bitches have a B.H.S. (beta haemolytic streptococcus) infection which will cause weak, fading puppies, but it is easily removed with a course of an appropriate antibiotic. I have my studs swabbed regularly too, because a visiting bitch could easily infect them. You should also check your bitch for hookworm.

Be prepared to travel a fair distance if need be. Do not select the nearest stud simply because it happens to be conveniently close to home.

MATING

So now you have chosen the dog and booked the provisional mating with the owner. Stud fees are usually the price of a pet puppy, but may vary from country to country and according to the dog's merit. Be sure you know the stud fee well in advance as it is normally paid at the time of the service, although some people will accept a puppy in lieu of a stud fee.

I like to try the bitch about the tenth day from the first signs of season – this may be too early for some bitches, but some are ovulating at this time and the correct day varies from bitch to bitch. If she will not 'stand' for the dog, then try her on the twelfth day and again on the fourteenth day. When a bitch is ready she will allow the dog to lick her vulva with evident enjoyment and will curl her tail to one side. Some maiden bitches will love the preliminaries but snap if the dog tries to mount them. This is where the stud owner (usually an experienced breeder) must define whether your bitch is just being 'touch me not', is not ready, or is past the correct time. I find that my own male dogs tell me if a bitch is ready or not by their attitude and behaviour. Sometimes the bitch

Top: *The dogs will become acquainted by engaging in a playful 'courting' session.*

Middle: *The bitch will signal her willingness to mate by presenting her rear end to the dog.*

Bottom: *The dog will mount the bitch and effect a 'tie', with his penis swelling inside her.*

Right: *The dog will then turn his back to the bitch. A maiden bitch may panic, so hold her firmly by the collar.*

Below: *The dogs will remain in the mating position for 5 – 45 minutes. Do not let them wander about during this period.*

is willing to mate if the owner is not looking. It sounds silly, but there are bitches who are so 'humanized' and devoid of instinct that they think it is naughty to allow such liberties.

It is important that the dog 'courts' the bitch. A little foreplay will often stimulate the bitch but too much will tire out the dog, so let them just get to know each other. When the dog actually mounts the bitch, hold her collar so that she does not turn and snap at the crucial moment. A collar is important when mating a bitch, as you need something more solid than a check chain to hang on to. Once the dog has entered the bitch he will swell up inside her and effect a 'tie', so that they cannot part until the dog's penis has gone down again. Some maiden bitches panic, so it is important to hold her firmly and not let her thrash about, which could damage her

and the dog. The male will turn round until they are back to back and there they remain for 5-45 minutes, until the 'tie' is over. It is always advisable to hold them both at this point as they will often attempt to wander about in this position and make themselves very uncomfortable.

Once the pair have separated a fair amount of fluid will come out of the bitch. Do not worry, as this is just flushing fluid – the actual semen is well on its way to do the job. There is absolutely no need to hold up the bitch's back legs like a wheelbarrow, as I have seen some people do or, even worse, spit on the hand and slap it on the bitch's vulva to 'seal it'.

It is advisable to have two matings about 48 hours apart. This will ensure the fertilization of the eggs, since the sperm lives for at least 24 hours within the bitch and so this covers you for at least a four day period.

WHELPING

Until the bitch starts to show 'in whelp' at about five to six weeks treat her as normal, giving perhaps a little extra calcium and vitamin supplement. Later on she will have to have smaller meals and be fed twice or even thrice daily. Be sure that she has good nourishing food, but do not let her pack on the fat. Walks will be steadier as she will not feel like leaping about, so let her go at her own pace and keep her fit.

Your whelping area should be ready, with the whelping box in place, and she should be encouraged to use the area and box to sleep in. Some bitches dig holes when pregnant. This is the nest-building instinct at work, so do not scold her if she digs up your flowers – the force telling her to do it is very strong and she will become upset. Just plant a few more flowers and see things in perspective.

As the sixty-third day approaches you may see a white mucus discharge from the vulva. This is normal so do not worry. The temperature of the bitch will drop from 101°F (38°C) to 99°F (37°C) or 98°F (36.5°C) the day before whelping, and she will tear up her bedding. Some bitches refuse to eat the day before whelping but Rottweilers are often so greedy that they eat as normal. Have a bottle of

disinfectant for sterilizing, clean towels, scissors and lots of clean newspapers in readiness for the birth, plus a cardboard box and a hot water bottle just in case you need it for the puppies. It is a good idea to tell your vet when the bitch is due so that he can be on standby if needed. I usually have a pack of puppy milk and a baby's bottle and teat just in case her milk is late, or she needs help with feeding a large litter.

As zero hour approaches the bitch will be restless, panting, tearing up her bed, circling round and looking at her rear end apprehensively, interspersed with periods of calm. It is essential that you do not get nervous; sit quietly with her,

speaking in a calm, confident voice, watch and wait. Do not invite in the neighbours to spectate, and do not rush about and panic – this is a normal, natural event and your little expectant mum will do a good job so long as you do not fuss too much. The first sign of an approaching puppy will be some strong pushes from the bitch, followed soon after by either a bubble of foetal membrane or the pup itself. Most bitches expel their pups easily, but some will be born hindfirst and you may well have to grip the back legs of the pup with a clean towel and wait until the next push before *gently* helping the pup into the world. Most births in this breed are relatively easy but a useful tip is not to let the bitch go more than three hours between pups if she is straining and pushing. This usually means problems, so call your vet.

When the pup is born the bitch will bite the cord, eat the placenta and clean up the pup. Sometimes maiden bitches will not do this, so cut the cord with sterile scissors and rub the pup with a clean towel, giving it a little shake nose down to remove any mucus from the nasal passages, then present the pup to the mother again. If she is not interested, pop the puppy into a cardboard box with a clean towel over a hot water bottle and put it in a warm place – she will accept it later on when she has finished whelping. You may have to give her a firm command to lie down and let them all suckel, but she will soon settle as long as you do not interfere too much. Newly born pups need heat and food, and cannot urinate or defecate without stimulation, hence the mother's constant licking.

Left: *A pregnant bitch becoming accustomed to the whelping box. Note the 'pig rail' to prevent the mother from accidentally squashing the pups.*

THE FIRST WEEKS

Your bitch will need light, milky feeds with scrambled eggs and a little cereal for the first few days. Do not worry if she has loose black motions, as this is the normal result of eating the afterbirths (placentas), which are very rich in iron. Make sure she always has water to drink – lactating bitches need a lot of fluids and, as the pups grow, increase her food intake and provide plenty of milk as well. Some of my bitches almost treble their normal food intake spread over two or three meals when they are feeding pups. It is sensible to let the vet check her over after the birth to ensure that there are no retained puppies or

Below: *Mothers stand to give milk during the latter stage of the lactation period.*

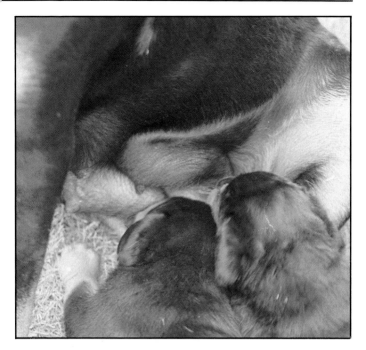

Above: *Their mother's milk is best for puppies, providing them with vital nutrients.*

placentas which would quickly cause her temperature to rise and can create great problems. At this point, ask the vet to check the pups for malformations, such as cleft palates, or other problems.

At three to four days the tails need to be docked and the dew claws removed. I use the elastic band method for docking, tying the band tightly round the tail as close to the body as possible, but checking that the band is not on the ring of wrinkled skin round the anus. The dew claws I remove with sharp sterilized scissors, puffing on an antibiotic powder to prevent infection and clot the blood quickly. If in doubt ask your vet or an experienced breeder to do it as it is not really a novice's job. It is best to take your bitch out when this is done as it will upset her.

You may find that one or two pups are pushed to a far corner of the box by their mother and they usually appear to be cold and feeble. I wish I could tell you that they will be all right but

usually, if the mother rejects them, there is a reason – they do not smell right and she knows better than us. I never try to revive feeble puppies. If they are not robust and healthy, do you really want to keep pups which are likely to be sickly, weedy dogs? In a very large litter you have a choice either to cull some of them or bottle feed at two-hourly intervals, since some will die anyway from lack of food.

Bottle feeding is hard work and, as the pups get maternal immunity from the colostrum, or first milk, they all need to have it. It is best to feed half the litter on bottle milk for one feed and allow the other half to feed from the mother, then alternate at the next feed, making sure that every pup gets that essential mother's milk. The bitch still needs peace and quiet at this stage, so do not bring friends and relatives in to view the pups until they are older, or she will become agitated.

At three weeks of age you can start to wean a large litter (four weeks if it is a small one). Begin with a little milky cereal – finely ground oats with an egg yolk or two is good – or scrambled egg.

The pups will make a mess at first but within two or three days they will get used to eating. Food for weaning must be like a purée with no lumps. At six weeks your puppies will eat minced cooked meat and cereal or flaked fish with cereal, and you can use cooked eggs, too. Four feeds a

Left: *A good mother checking up on two of her puppies. In their game they are showing typical dominant/submissive postures.*

Above: *For the first eight weeks the mother dominates the puppy's life; after this the puppy can be found a new home.*

day are required and do not forget to give puppy milk or fresh goats' milk as cows' milk will often scour them for some reason. Always remember the golden rule – do not let them get fat. People ask what they should weigh at various ages and I have heard all sorts of answers to this question. My own view is that if they look good, well-covered but not fat, if they eat well and have lots of energy, and if they are well-boned and healthy, they are the right weight. If you develop a good eye for livestock you should see for yourself what physical condition they are in.

Worm them at four, six and eight weeks and pick up the puppies' droppings several times a day, especially when they have just been wormed. If you do not do this the pups will roll over in droppings when they play and

get very smelly and messy, and may also become re-infected.

The pups will be ready to go to their new homes at eight weeks. When prospective owners come, check that they have a responsible person at home all day and that they have a large outside area which is well fenced. Do not forget to tell them all the problems which can arise in this breed and how to deal with them, and – very important – check that the prospective owners have firm, sensible temperaments and want the dog for the right reasons.

Give a diet sheet (see p.88), and perhaps even a few days' supply of the food to which the puppy is used. If your registrations are back from the Kennel Club be sure to give them, as well as the pedigree; if not, send them on later.

Chapter Six

FEEDING AND CARE

Obesity
Grooming
Worming
Line and inbreeding

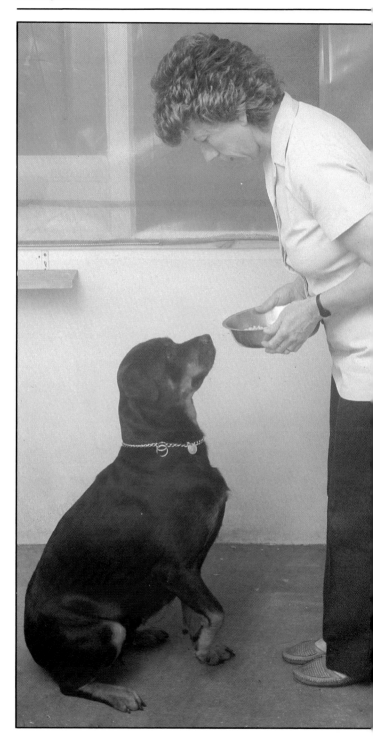

OBESITY

Within any breed there are dogs that need more or less food than others, and the Rottweiler is no exception. For example, a dog which lies around the house all day will need fewer calories than a breeding animal or a dog which works or takes a great deal of exercise. My daughter has a large stable of horses and her Rottweiler does over 20 miles (32km) a day accompanying rides: he is quite a small male (about 25in (63cm) to the shoulder) but he eats far more than my house male 'Max', who is very much bigger.

It is important, therefore, to calculate roughly how many calories your own dog needs. A good rule is the less exercise, the less food. Most pet Rottweilers are much too fat: their owners are cutting their lifespan with overfeeding or, as my father used to say, 'letting them dig their own grave with their teeth!' It is a sad fact that people seldom realize or accept that their dog is fat; the wisest way is to consult your vet if you want an honest opinion.

Most vets hate obesity in animals, much preferring to see a dog really lean and this is only common sense, because fatness brings a whole set of problems. Try to look at your dog dispassionately. Can you feel its ribs easily? If not, it is probably too fat. You can buy obesity diets from your vet or you can cut the dog's carbohydrate ration in half and gradually step up the amount of exercise he gets. Within three months you will have a much fitter dog. I give my dogs a fasting day every now and then if I see extra pounds creeping on – it helps a lot.

One often sees advertisements for puppies where the father is

stated to be 15 stones (210 lb, 95kg) and the mother 13 stones (182lb, 83kg). It is absolutely crazy to allow Rottweilers to reach that kind of weight. Remember always that this is a working breed, not a contender for the best beef cattle at a stock show!

So what should we feed our dogs? Scientists and nutritionists tell us that the average dog can manage very well on about 18 – 20 per cent of protein daily, so various companies manufacture well-formulated dried foods which you can mix with water to give a good diet. There are dozens of these all-in-one diets and it is important to select one which suits your dog. The one I use is 19.5 per cent protein: it is fortified with vitamins and minerals and I find my dogs do really well on it, so I never give them a change of diet since any changes are liable to cause loose motions.

It is only a human idea to give dogs variety in diet: in the wild there would not be much diversity – just some meat, bones and offal every day. Nowadays, with protein so expensive, it is sensible to cut down on meat and give cheaper forms of protein. As long as the dogs do well on it, there should be no problem. For example, I would feed an adult male Rottweiler taking moderate exercise about three-quarters all-in-one diet to one-quarter protein (this can be fish, hard boiled eggs or pet mince).

In the winter dogs which live outside need more food (and deeper, warmer bedding) to keep out the cold. I do not mind if mine are a few pounds overweight in winter, but come the springtime I adjust their diet until they look good again.

A growing puppy at eight weeks I feed all-in-one, mixed with a good quality puppy milk or goats' milk for the first feed. The next feed is two-thirds all-in-one, well soaked in gravy, to one-third protein (fish, eggs or meat). Then I repeat these two feeds for the third and fourth meals, with a little vitamin and mineral supplement added to the latter (less than it tells you on the pack since the all-in-one is already fortified).

A rough guide as to quantities: as I suggested earlier, feed about the size of the dog's head per meal. This works well until you get a dog with either a really overdone huge head or a tiny pin-head. In either case you use common sense again, giving the huge headed one a little less and the pin-head a little more. I never weigh anything – food, dogs or pups – since I like to gauge by eye. If the dog looks good, is fit not fat, and has lots of energy, then you are feeding correctly. There is no time in my day to be forever weighing things; if I have some spare time then I prefer to spend it either training or playing with a pup.

At three months the puppies go on to three feeds a day (obviously slightly larger quantities) and at six months two feeds of even larger quantities per meal. At one year the ration is one meal daily, although this may vary according to the dog's needs. Pregnant bitches, as they advance into their sixth or seventh week, need to eat twice or sometimes three times daily as the pups take up a lot of room and the stomach cannot expand as much. Don't forget that Rottweilers in general are very greedy and will often insist that they just have to have that sandwich you are eating or they will fade away and die from starvation! Don't give in to such transparent lies; don't feed between meals and don't buy 'choc drops' or other junk foods for your dog. If you want to give the dog a real treat, buy marrow bones for it or go out for an extra walk – better for you and far better for the dog.

Another food popular with dog owners is tripe (beef stomach).

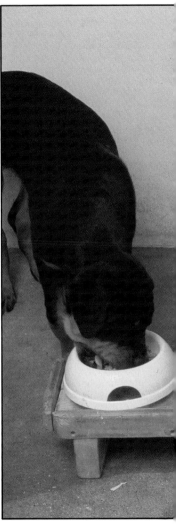

This is fine, as long as you remember that tripe is lacking in the essential minerals – calcium and iron; can contain a lot of fat and is not suitable as a complete diet. If you use it, you must give carbohydrate and add the iron and calcium it lacks, so provide a chunk of cooked liver daily and a tablespoonful of bone meal, together with some wholemeal biscuit or all-in-one meal. I never use tripe to feed pups as I like to fill them with good, nourishing, growing food, and tripe is not the

Above: *Feed your puppies from individual dishes to ensure fair distribution. A table will discourage the pups from turning out their feet.*

best for this purpose.

Raw meat, especially lamb or pork, is very dangerous as it can give your dog tapeworm, porcine herpes virus or salmonella poisoning. Always bring meat to the boil to sterilize it and never ever feed bones which are liable to splinter, causing perforation of the dog's gut. Be careful to boil the meat thoroughly. Part boiling wil do no good. A pressure cooker is useful to boil down fish pieces and you can even feed the bones as they will be almost disintegrated by pressure cooking. This is a good source of calcium. Breast of lamb is good cooked in this way as the bones go soft; you can skim off the fat and feed all the rest.

Canned meats mixed with biscuit are very popular, but I

89

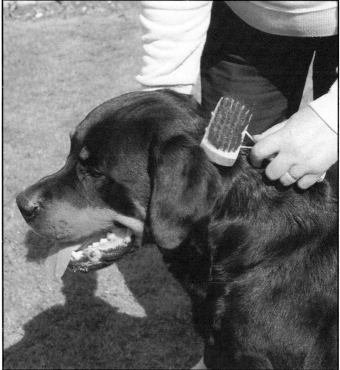

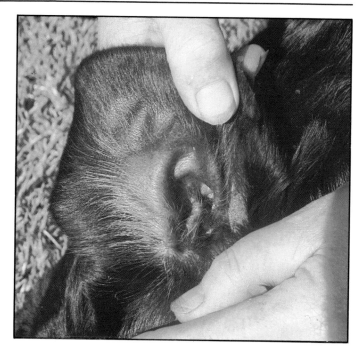

Above: *Check inside the ears every week for embedded grass seeds or signs of ear mites. Both can cause trouble.*

Top left: *Give your dog a good brush every week to keep the coat shining. During the moult, groom every day.*

Bottom left: *A double-sided brush, with wire on one side and rubber bristles on the other, is an ideal grooming tool.*

find this diet very expensive and, in my own dogs, it causes a great deal of flatulence, so I have to give charcoal granules to combat this.

Adult Rottweilers can have table scraps added to their meal, and if you have any stale wholemeal bread pop it into the oven until it bakes hard – they love it! If you want to keep a glossy coat on your dog, give a small piece of polyunsaturated margarine daily (about the size of the top of your little finger).

Never feed sugary substances and don't allow your dog to develop a sweet tooth. Mine will not eat sweets as they have never formed a liking for them, and that's the way I like to keep things.

Some Rottweilers have a taste for fruit and this means they must need extra Vitamin C, so give them a little fruit (for example orange) daily. I have one dog who would eat several oranges if I let him, and he adores melon, too.

GROOMING

I have found that if you feed well you need only give the dog a good brush weekly to keep the coat shining, although during the moult it is as well to have a daily grooming session to remove the dead hair. A rubber cat brush works well and, during the moult, I gently use a metal claw brush to take out dead undercoat, finishing off with a damp chamois leather to add a glossy finish to the coat.

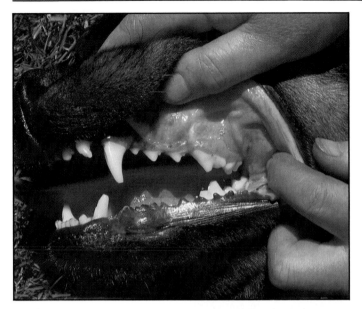

Ears need to be examined weekly for signs of ear mites and a drop or two of a good anti-mite lotion (from your vet) inserted if there are any brown secretions.

If your dog's teeth are full of tartar you can use a toothbrush and doggy toothpaste. I find most dogs hate this procedure, but will put up with it. However, I use the edge of a milled coin to scrape it off very gently, taking care not to make the gums bleed. Marrow bones will prevent much of this problem because the very act of eating them removes such deposits on the teeth. In extreme cases your vet will clean the teeth, possibly with the aid of an anaesthetic for difficult dogs.

If your dog has good feet you will never need to cut the claws; sadly, not all do and some dogs need to have the claws trimmed from time to time. Use the guillotine-type clippers, which do not pinch the quick of the nail. The claws on Rottweilers are black and you cannot see the quick, so a little and often is better than cutting a lot and making the quick bleed. If it does don't worry, as the bleeding will soon stop. You can puff a little

Top: *Your dog's teeth should be checked regularly for tartar. A serious build-up could mean a visit to the vet.*

Above: *Claws are best cut using a pair of guillotine clippers. They cause a dog the minimum of aggravation.*

sulphonilamide powder on the claw to help the blood clot and prevent infection, or you can use friar's balsam. Some people file their dog's claws with a rasp, but I find that clipping is easier for the dog. Exercise on hard surfaces also helps to keep claws short, so try road walking. This also tones up the muscles, especially if it is done at a brisk pace and not an amble.

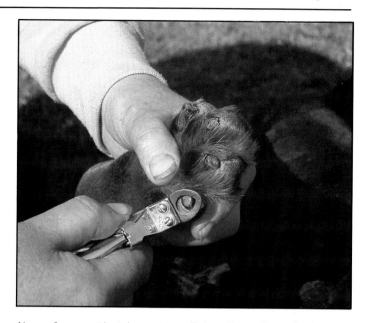

Above: *Care must be taken not to cut the claw's quick. To avoid making it bleed, trim only a little off at a time.*

Below: *If your Rottweiler has been bred with good tight feet, then cutting claws should never really be necessary.*

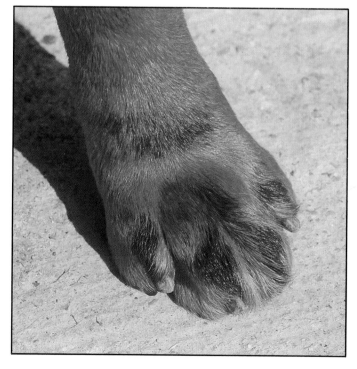

EXERCISING

It is very common in Europe for owners to ride bicycles, the dog following behind, but there is a tendency to do too much too soon. *Never* take a Rottweiler out with a bicycle until it is over one year old and already in good condition: do just a little daily until it is really fit, and make sure that you keep the dog away from danger, such as traffic.

There is one handler/owner in Germany who is well over 60 years old, and he jogs with his dog for two hours daily. They are a joy to see in the show ring, both supremely fit and bursting with health and vitality; they can easily outrun most other Rottweilers and handlers and the rapport between them is wonderful.

But remember, no hard exercise until that first year is over, and get your dog fit gradually. There is a section of the population which leaves the dog lounging around the house all week, then goes for five-hour runs at weekends. They are surprised when their dog cannot walk properly on Monday morning.

This breed is not demanding of exercise, but they do enjoy it, so try to make time each day for you and your dog to have a walk or two.

WORMING

Worming needs to be done on a regular basis and during puppyhood it should take place several times, since roundworms

Below: *Puppies playing in the garden at will can rest when they become tired.*

will keep a puppy in poor shape at best and kill it at worst. Adults should be wormed every three months, since they can pick up roundworm larvae from sniffing the excrement of other dogs. It is cheap and easy to worm a dog and it is always best to buy a medicine from your vet.

The public outcry of late about roundworm larvae causing blindness in children does have basis in fact, but do not panic. If your dog is wormed regularly the chance of your child suffering is about the same as the chance of it being sat on by an elephant! Naturally, do not let your dog lick the child's mouth or hands, and make the child wash the hands if they have been licked.

Tapeworm, which is transmitted by fleas and raw meat, affects some dogs. It looks like grains of rice adhering to the dog's anal area and when you see them go straight to the vet

and dose for tapeworm. There is no disgrace in having them, but there is disgrace in leaving them there!

Heartworm, transmitted by mosquitoes, is a problem in some countries. This needs a daily pill to keep it away – consult your vet as to the vermicides required for your area.

Check a bitch for hookworms before breeding from her. These can be deadly if passed on to pups and are very debilitating in older dogs; veterinary care is essential to combat them.

Never ignore worms: they cause a lot of problems, so it is always best to worm regularly as prevention is better than cure for both the dog and you.

Below: *An egg and the first larval stage of the roundworm. Worm regularly to ensure that your dog is free of them.*

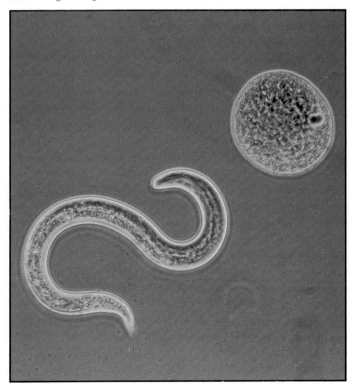

LINE AND INBREEDING

There is a great difference between line breeding and inbreeding. Line breeding is the selection of the best dogs in the line and breeding back to them, eg, granddaughter to grandson, or perhaps great-grandson to granddaughter, thus doubling up on the best lines. Below is the pedigree of a line bred bitch of mine which has produced a very good litter.

It is, however, very important when undertaking this to know what you are doing, and what the animals were like – inside and out. Doubling up on good temperament and good hips will not generally in my experience

Line breeding

PARENTS	GRANDPARENTS	GREAT GRANDPARENTS
SIRE Gamegards the Protector	SIRE The Fuhrer from Gamegards	SIRE Ch Gamegards Bulli v.d. Waldachquelle
		DAM Wandrin Shadow of Whitebeck
	DAM Gamegards Roman Road	SIRE Rohirrim Seiglinde
		DAM Gamegards the Coquette
DAM Gamegards the Witch	SIRE The Fuhrer from Gamegards	SIRE Ch Gamegards Bulli v.d. Waldachquelle
		DAM Wandrin Shadow of Whitebeck
	DAM Ch Schutz from Gamegards	SIRE Ch Gamegards Bulli v.d. Waldachquelle
		DAM Lohteyn Loyalty

Above: *This pedigree illustrates line-breeding. It is important that the dogs are HD-free and of good type and temperament.*

Left: *The author with several generations of Gamegards' Rottweilers, proving the benefits of good breeding.*

give bad temperament and bad hips, since you are reinforcing the genes for good qualities. Of course, you have to be sure that there are no recessive genes for bad qualities. A good thing about line breeding is that if there are recessive faults it will bring them to the fore. You will learn from it, and have greater knowledge of your bloodlines and what they reproduce.

You are doubling up on what is there – good and bad – so know the dogs in the line intimately, their faults and virtues. Some character faults to avoid in this method of breeding are hyperactivity, over-sensitivity to touch or sound, over-aggression, nervousness, biting, dullness or sluggishness. Only line breed to sterling characters which are sound mentally and physically. If you are not sure, do not do it.

Inbreeding is very close mating, ie brother to sister, father to daughter, etc. It is not a practice I use since you can make terrible mistakes if you do not know what the dogs carry genetically; you also tend to lose hybrid vigour if you do not expand your gene pool. Though some great champions in other breeds have been bred in this fashion with no ill effects, I think line breeding is a much safer procedure.

Chapter Seven

SHOWING AND COMPETITIVE TRAINING

The Breed Standards
Showing
Obedience shows

THE ROTTWEILER BREED STANDARDS

Below are both the British and American Rottweiler Breed Standards. Study them well if you want to learn about the breed.

ROTTWEILER BRITISH STANDARD

GENERAL APPEARANCE: Above average size, stalwart, dog. Correctly proportioned, compact and powerful form, permitting great strength, manoeuvrability and endurance.

CHARACTERISTICS: Appearance displays boldness and courage. Self assured and fearless. Calm gaze should indicate good humour.

TEMPERAMENT: Good natured, not nervous, aggressive or vicious; courageous, biddable, with natural guarding instincts.

HEAD AND SKULL: Head medium length, skull broad between ears. Forehead moderately arched as seen from side. Occipital bone well developed but not conspicuous. Cheeks well boned and muscled but not prominent. Skin on head not loose, although it may form a moderate wrinkle when attentive. Muzzle fairly deep with top line level, and length of muzzle in relation to distance from well-defined stop, to be as 2:3. Nose well developed with proportionately large nostrils, always black.

EYES: Medium size, almond-shaped, dark brown in colour, light eye undesirable, eyelids close-fitting.

MOUTH: Teeth strong, complete dentition with scissor bite, ie upper teeth closely overlapping the lower teeth and set square to the jaws. Flews (the fleshy upper lips) black and firm, falling gradually away towards corners of mouth, which do not protrude excessively.

EARS: Pendant, small in proportion rather than large, set high and wide apart, lying flat and close to neck.

NECK: Of fair length, strong, round and very muscular. Slightly arched, free from throatiness.

FOREQUARTERS: Shoulders well laid back, long and sloping, elbows well let down, but not loose. Legs straight, muscular, with plenty of bone and substance. Pasterns sloping slightly forward.

Above right: A stylized diagram of a male Rottweiler showing the points of conformation together with their names.

Below right: The Rottweiler, as a working dog, has a skeleton built for strength and stamina. Note particularly the sturdy legs, solid shoulder and roomy chest.

Skeleton	Conformation points
1 Skull	
2 Occiput	A Skull
3 Cervical vertebrae	B Withers
	C Loin
4 Scapula	D Rump
5 Thoracic vertebrae	E Stifle
	F Hock
6 Lumbar vertebrae	G Underline
	H Forearm
7 Pelvis	I Pastern
8 Femur	J Digits
9 Fibula	K Shoulder
10 Tibia	L Cheek
11 Tarsus	M Flews
12 Metatarsus	N Underjaw
13 Phalanges	O Muzzle
14 Ribs	P Stop
15 Ulna	
16 Radius	
17 Carpus	
18 Metacarpus	
19 Humerus	
20 Mandible	

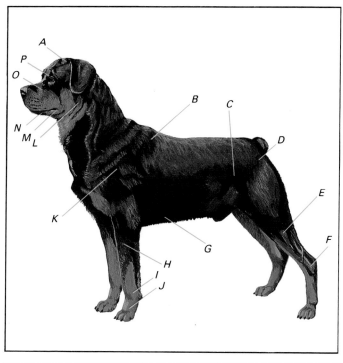

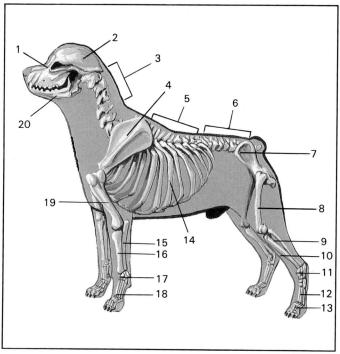

BODY: Chest roomy, broad and deep with well-sprung ribs. Depth of brisket will be not more, and not much less, than 50 per cent of shoulder height. Back straight, strong and not too long, ratio of shoulder height to length of body should be 9:10, loins short, strong and deep, flanks not tucked up. Croup of proportionate length, and broad, very slightly sloping.

HINDQUARTERS: Upper thigh broad, strongly muscled and not too short. Lower thigh well-muscled at top, strong and sinewy below. Stifles fairly well bent. Hocks well angulated without exaggeration, metatarsals not completely vertical. Strength and soundness of hock highly desirable.

FEET: Strong, round and compact with toes well arched. Hind feet somewhat longer than front. Pads very hard, toenails short, dark and strong. Rear dewclaws removed.

TAIL: Normally carried horizontally, but slightly above horizontal when dog is alert. Customarily docked at first joint, it is strong and not set too low.

GAIT/MOVEMENT: Conveys an impression of supple strength, endurance and purpose. While back remains firm and stable there is a powerful hindthrust and good stride. First and foremost, movement should be harmonious, positive and unrestricted.

COAT: Double top coat is of medium length, coarse and flat. Undercoat, essential on the neck and thighs, should not show through top coat. Hair may be a little longer on the back of the forelegs and breechings (back of the upper thigh). Long or excessively wavy coat highly undesirable.

COLOUR: Black with clearly

Above: *The head should be of medium length with a broad skull and a slightly arching forehead.*

defined markings as follows: a spot over each eye, on cheeks, as a strip around each side of muzzle (but not on bridge of nose), on throat, two clear triangles on either side of the breast bone, on forelegs from carpus downward to toes, on inside of rear legs from hock to toes (but not completely eliminating black of legs), under tail. Colour or markings from rich tan to mahogany; they should not exceed 10 per cent of body colour. White marking is highly undesirable. Black pencil markings on toes is desirable. Undercoat is grey, fawn, or black.

SIZE: Dog's height at shoulder between 25–27in (63–69cm) Bitches between 23–25in (58–63.5cm). Height should always be considered in relation to general appearance.

FAULTS: Any departure from the foregoing points should be considered a fault and the seriousness with which the fault should be regarded should be in exact proportion to its degree.

NOTE: Male animals should have two apparently normal testicles fully descended into the scrotum.

ROTTWEILER
AMERICAN STANDARD

GENERAL APPEARANCE: The ideal Rottweiler is a large, robust and powerful dog, black with clearly defined rust markings. His compact build denotes great strength, agility and endurance. Males are characteristically larger, heavier boned and more masculine in appearance.

SIZE: Males 24–27in (61–69cm) Females 22–25in (56–63.5cm) Proportion should always be considered rather than height alone. The length of the body, from breast bone (sternum) to rear edge of pelvis (ischium), is slightly longer than the height of the dog at the withers; the most desirable proportion being 10:9. Depth of chest should be 50 per cent of height. Serious faults: lack of proportion, undersize, oversize.

HEAD: Of medium length, broad between ears; forehead line seen

Below: *The American Standard demands a build capable of strength and agility.*

in profile is moderately arched. Cheekbones and stop well developed; length of muzzle should not exceed distance between stop and occiput. Skull is preferred dry; however, some wrinkling may occur when dog is alert.

MUZZLE: Bridge is straight, broad at base with slight tapering towards tip. Nose is broad rather than round, with black nostrils.

LIPS: Always black; corners tightly closed. Inner mouth pigment is dark. A pink mouth is to be penalized.

TEETH: Forty-two in number (20

Above: *The bridge of the muzzle should be straight; the nose should be broad and black.*

upper and 22 lower); strong, correctly placed, meeting in a scissors bite – lower incisors touching inside of upper incisors. Serious faults: any missing tooth, level bite. Disqualifications: undershot, overshot, four or more missing teeth.

EYES: Of medium size, moderately deep-set, almond-shaped, with well-fitting lids. Iris of uniform colour, from medium to dark brown, the darker shade

Above: *The eyes should be medium in size, dark brown in colour and almond-shaped, with well-fitting lids.*

always preferred. Serious faults: yellow (bird of prey) eyes, eyes not of same colour, eyes unequal in size or shape, hairless lid.

EARS: Pendant, proportionately small, triangular in shape; set well apart and placed on skull so as to make it appear broader when the dog is alert. Ear terminates at approximately mid cheek level. Correctly held, the inner edge will lie tightly against cheek.

NECK: Powerful, well muscled, moderately long with slight arch and without loose skin.

BODY: Topline is firm and level, extending in straight line from withers to croup. Brisket deep, reaching to elbow, chest roomy, broad with well pronounced forechest. Ribs should be well-sprung. Loin short, deep and well muscled. Croup broad, medium length, slightly sloping.

TAIL: Normally carried in horizontal position, giving impression of an elongation of top line. Carried slightly above horizontal when dog is excited. Some dogs are born without a

105

tail, or with a very short stub. Tail is normally docked short close to the body. The set of the tail is more important than length.

FOREQUARTERS: Shoulder blade long, well laid back at 45° angle. Elbows tight, well under

body. Distance from withers to elbow and elbow to ground is equal. Legs strongly developed

Below: The upper thigh should be broad and well-muscled; look for a strong hock and thigh.

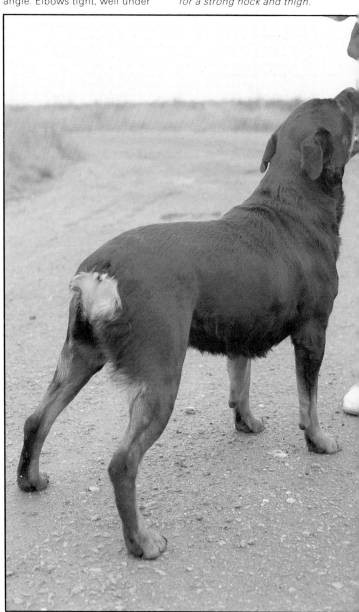

with straight heavy bone, not set closely together. Pasterns strong, springy and almost perpendicular to ground. Feet round, compact, well-arched toes, turning neither in nor out. Pads thick and hard; nails short, strong and black. Dewclaws may be removed.

HINDQUARTERS: Angulation of hindquarters balances that of forequarters. Upper thigh fairly long, broad and well muscled. Stifle joint moderately angulated. Lower thigh long, powerful, extensively muscled, leading into a strong hock joint; metatarsus nearly perpendicular to ground. Viewed from rear, hind legs are straight and wide enough apart to fit in with a properly built body. Feet somewhat longer than front feet, well-arched toes turning neither in nor out. Dewclaws must be removed if present.

COAT: Outer coat is straight, coarse, dense, medium length, lying flat. Undercoat must be present on neck and thighs, but should not show through the outer coat. The Rottweiler should be exhibited in a natural condition without trimming, except to remove whiskers, if desired. Fault: wavy coat. Serious faults: excessively short coat, curly or open coat; lack of undercoat. Disqualification: long coat.

COLOUR: Always black with rust to mahogany markings. The borderline between black and rust should be clearly defined. The markings should be located as follows: a spot over each eye; on cheeks, as a strip around each side of the muzzle, but not on the bridge of nose; on throat; triangular mark on either side of breastbone; on forelegs from carpus downward to toes; on inside of rear legs showing down the front of stifle and broadening out to front of rear legs from hock to toes, but not completely eliminating black from back of legs; under tail. Black pencil markings on toes. The undercoat is grey or black. Quantity and location of rust markings is important and should not exceed 10 per cent of body colour. Insufficient or excessive markings should be penalized. Serious faults: excessive markings; white markings any place on dog (a few white hairs do not constitute a marking); light coloured markings. Disqualification: any base colour other than black; total absence of markings.

GAIT: The Rottweiler is a trotter. The motion is harmonious, sure, powerful and unhindered, with a strong fore-reach and a powerful rear drive. Front and rear legs are thrown neither in nor out, as the imprint of hind feet should touch that of forefeet. In a trot, the forequarters and hindquarters are mutually co-ordinated while the back remains firm; as speed is increased, legs will converge under body towards a centre line.

CHARACTER: The Rottweiler should possess a fearless expression with a self-assured aloofness that does not lend itself to immediate and indiscriminate friendships. He has an inherent desire to protect home and family, and is an intelligent dog of extreme hardness and adaptability with a strong willingness to work. A judge shall dismiss from the ring any shy or vicious Rottweiler. Shyness: a dog shall be judged fundamentally shy if, refusing to stand for examination, it shrinks away from the judge; if it fears an approach from the rear; if it shies at sudden or unusual noises to a marked degree. Viciousness: a dog that attacks or attempts to attack either the judge or its handler is definitely vicious. An aggressive or belligerent attitude towards other dogs shall not be deemed viciousness.

SHOWING

The history books tell us that the Rottweiler was first shown in competition in 1882 in Heilbronn in Germany. On that day only one dog entered, though history doesn't tell us how well it did. Things, however, have changed a great deal since then, and often not for the better.

Due to the population explosion of this breed there seem to be some people judging Rottweilers who are very inexperienced. This is a problem which one hopes will be overcome in time, when they gain the knowledge required. Sadly, many new judges think that after owning Rottweilers for a few years they are experts, whereas it is only by keeping an open mind and continuing to learn over many years that one becomes an expert – and even experts, if wise, never stop learning. Beware the instant expert judges, the judges who are rough or over-handle the dogs, and the judges who have so little confidence in their own judgement that they put up only well-known, or their friends', dogs.

How do you select your shows and judges? I am afraid that it is by trial and error; by attending shows under a variety of judges you will soon learn which ones to avoid. Shows are advertised in weekly or monthly dog magazines with the address and telephone number of the Show Secretary. If you contact them, they will send you a schedule with an entry form.

Having filled in your entry form and posted it off before the closing date, with the correct fee, you then put in a little extra show training. Daily sessions of about 5–10 minutes, teaching your dog to stand in a natural but flattering position, trot on a loose lead, and ignore other dogs, should have already taken place by the time you enter your first show. At the moment there is a silly fashion in Britain for the handler to stand in front of the dog with the handler's knee almost touching the dog's breastbone. This causes the dog to gaze up with the nose pointing skywards, masking the dog's front and spoiling the profile of the dog. Judges need to see the dog standing in a natural way with the head looking forward, not upward, showing off the lay of the shoulder and crest of the

Below: *In the show ring, ignoring other dogs is as important as performing a correct trot.*

Bottom: *A perfect show position should show off the front part of the dog: the lay of the shoulder and the neck.*

neck. The front of the dog should be clearly visible and a good handler should be almost invisible.

Teach your dog to walk into the 'stand' position on a loose lead, tell it to 'stay' and move back; you may use a titbit, but keep your hands down so that the dog is not looking up all the time.

Get various friends to 'go over' the dog for you, gently feeling the back, thighs and shoulders. If the dog gets upset upon examination, then go back to your 'stand stay' training and teach the dog to 'stand stay' no matter who touches it. It is wise to show the judge the dog's teeth yourself and if you have done your homework in teaching the dog to stand, and let you peel back the lips to expose the teeth, all will be well.

If your dog has heavy feathering on the hind legs and the tail has a few longish hairs, it is permissible to clip the long hair neatly so that the dog looks more clean cut.

Get to the show in good time so that your dog has a chance to settle in and go to the 'dog loo' area.

When you get into the ring, relax and enjoy it. Concentrate on displaying your dog to the best advantage; if you are placed, it is a nice bonus, but most of all, enjoy your day and be sure that your dog does too.

Do not leave your dog unattended on the bench, as

Show tips

Remember on show day to take:
(a) Collar, benching chain, water and bowl
(b) Ring card clips (you can buy these at most shows)
(c) Titbits (some people use a belt with a titbit bag on it)
(d) Brush, chamois leather
(e) Blanket for the bench (if it is a benched show)
(f) Exhibitor's passes

---

there have been dogs stolen or interfered with at some shows. Weirdos lurk everywhere and some show-goers become very nasty and spiteful if you win and they don't. Whatever happens, try to be a nice exhibitor and not one of the loud-mouthed varieties; be kind to others and don't crow if you win. Take a win or a beating with the same good grace. After all, it is the dog you love going home with you, be it a winner or a loser and who knows, things could be reversed next time out. If you want to leave your dog on the bench and look around the show, it is a good idea to make friends with another exhibitor and let them watch your dog, then you can offer to watch theirs in return.

Below: *Show benches can be made more comfortable with a blanket and water bowl.*

Never leave dogs in cars at shows – this has caused death on just moderately warm days. Do not chance it, as it is a horrible way for a dog to die. In America I have seen Rottweilers wearing wet towelling dog coats to keep them cool at shows on hot days. It is a good idea, since this breed is not at its best in extremely hot weather.

Working Trials are more difficult, but I find them much more enjoyable. The work is harder and more practical, there is less emphasis on precision and more on real working ability. CD (Companion Dog) class is:
1. Heel on lead
2. Heel free
3. Send away
4. Recall
5. Retrieve a dumbbell on the flat
6. Scale jump 6ft (1.8m)
7. Clear jump 3ft (0.9m)
8. Long jump 9ft (2.7m)
9. Sit Stay 2 minutes, handler out of sight
10. Down Stay 10 minutes, handler out of sight
11. Search an area of 15sq yd (12sq m) for four scented articles. You are allowed only four minutes for this exercise.

You must obtain half marks in each exercise to qualify, and this is what you are working towards, not necessarily to winning

In America, to qualify for the Companion Dog (CD) (Novice) class, the dog must score 170–200 points at three different American Kennel Club (AKC) shows. The dog must:
1. Heel on leash
2. Heel off leash
3. Stand for examination
4. Come on command
5. One minute sit stay
6. Three minute down stay

In my teens I did Working Trials with a red/white English Bull Terrier bitch and when she retired at eight years old I was sure I would never find another Bull Terrier which could jump like her. Having had Bull Terriers since childhood I could not find another breed I really wanted until I saw my first Rottweiler working – Mrs Mcphail's Rintelna the Bombadier CDEX UDEX. It was love at first sight and I was

Below: *Showing off how well a Rottweiler can work: taking the clear jump with lots to spare.*

Above: *A safer test of ability than the scale jump: an 'A' frame avoids a risky high drop.*

soon the proud owner of his son, Emil from Blackforest (Panzer). He was the best dog I have ever owned. As well as working and qualifying at trials, he did over 900 film and television parts.

Trialling is a rewarding pastime, but there is one big snag in Britain at the moment: the scale jump. It is very hard on a Rottweiler's shoulders, as coming down from 6ft (1.8m) is jarring and can cause serious injury. There are groups of people lobbying for an A frame at trials, as it is just as testing of agility and allows more breeds, such as Springer Spaniels, Bull Terriers and other, shorter-legged heavy dogs, to compete. Trials should be for everyone, not just the working breeds.

For the UD (Utility Dog) stake the dogs must do all the CD work, plus track a scent, and for each stake – WD (Working Dog), TD (Tracker Dog), up to PD (Police Dog) – the work becomes progressively more difficult. PD includes attack work as well, and even greater control exercises like recall from a fleeing criminal without biting, searching for a hidden person and speaking but not biting are taught. Those dogs which qualify PDEX have really been trained well and are totally under control.

For the show ring your dog must be clean and shining, fit not fat, and completely well-behaved at all times.

Showing is becoming a very serious business nowadays, and the days when I got tied to a tent post at Windsor Championship Show just before the Open Bitch Class for a joke are long gone. I was untied just in time to dash into the ring and win a first prize with my old Champion Schutz!

OBEDIENCE SHOWS

The rules of competitive obedience shows and trials vary from country to country, but let me tell you what a dog needs to do in Britain in, for example, Novice Obedience.

1. Heel on lead
2. Heel free
3. Retrieve a dumbbell on the flat
4. Recall to handler
5. Sit Stay 1 minute
6. Down Stay 3 minutes
7. Stand Stay
8. Temperament test on lead

The standard is very high, with the fast, super-attentive Border Collies being very hard to beat. You need great precision in obedience in order to win, and must practise very hard under expert guidance. Join the best dog obedience class you can find, making sure that the instructors really know their job. Some instructors go off on a month's course and come back with a piece of paper which says 'You are now a dog trainer'. That's fine, but you should establish that they really do have practical experience. What have they won? Have they worked any other dog than a Border Collie or German Shepherd? Watch them carefully with their own dogs: are the animals happy, willing workers? Can the instructor tell you in simple terms what you need to know?

If you get a good instructor and attend a good club he or she will soon point out your faults and help you to achieve better results. There is not enough space here for a full guide on

Top: *The chase begins. Attack work requires total obedience and strict training. It should never be taught unnecessarily.*

Right: *The man has failed to outrun the dog, and the dog strikes. Note the leather protection on the man's arm.*

Top: *The dog will hold the 'criminal' until given the release command by the handler.*

competitive training – it needs a book all to itself, so I have included a list of titles at the back of this book.

I am against members of the general public teaching their dogs to attack, as you need to have incredible obedience and control before you do this and very few people can be bothered to do all the hard work of the control exercises. Some people are eager to have a Rottweiler which attacks but do not have the discipline to put into it, and this can be highly dangerous. I will give you an example of the sort of thing which happened to me with my 'Panzer'.

I was meeting my ex-husband; he came out of a doorway in a crowd of people when the dog and I were some distance away and I told 'Panzer' to go and meet him, letting the dog off the leash to go. Just at that moment a man came out of the crowd and began to run fast, away from us. Panzer, who was attack trained, made a misjudgement and misinterpreted my command. As the dog went into top gear I realized what had happened and

yelled 'Down Panzer!' Fortunately we had done our control exercises and the dog dropped down about three paces from the running man who, incidentally, was totally unaware that behind him was a Rottweiler intent on grabbing him. The man went on his way and I recalled the dog, but just imagine what could have happened had the dog not been obedient. Such incidents can occur with an attack trained dog, so you see why the control is so important.

The Rottweiler can bite much harder than, say, a German Shepherd or a Doberman and can inflict terrible damage. I have seen the scars of such bites and they are not a pretty sight, so please do not encourage an untrained Rottweiler to bite anyone. Your Rottweiler has an inbuilt guarding instinct and, when mature, will protect you well, although just the fact that you have a Rottweiler by your side will deter most wrongdoers.

I hope that you will do some training work with your dog, since it is one of the most rewarding pastimes and pays dividends in everyday life. You need only some spare time, a dog, and a little know how to have a whole new set of experiences opened up for you.

Appendix I

Glossary of dog terminology

Almond eyes: Oval-shaped like an almond, slanted at corners.

Angulation: Angle created by two joining bones; particularly, the shoulder and hock.

Bad mouth: Teeth crooked or misaligned overshot or undershot bite.

Barrel hocks: Turned-out hocks, (also called spread hocks, or divergent hocks).

Bench show: A show at which the dogs are 'benched' (leashed on benches).

Best in Show: The animal judged to be the best of all the breeds in a show.

Bitch: A female dog.

Bite: The position of the teeth when the mouth is shut.

Blanket: The coat colour on the back and upper part of the sides.

Blooded: Of good breeding; pedigreed.

Board: To kennel and care for a dog in its owner's absence, for a fee.

Bobtail: A tailless dog, or a dog with a very short docked tail.

Bodied up: Well-developed.

Bone: A well-boned dog is one with limbs that give an appearance and feel of strength and spring without coarseness.

Bossy: With over-development of the shoulder muscles.

Brace: A pair of dogs of the same type.

Breastbone: Bone running down the middle of the chest, to which all but the floating ribs are attached.

Breed: A variety of purebred dog; a dog or bitch with a pedigree.

Breeder: Someone who breeds dogs.

Breeding particulars: Sire, dam, date of birth, sex, colour, Kennel Club registration details, etc.

Brisket: The part of the lower chest that includes the breastbone.

Brood bitch: A bitch kept for breeding.

Burr: The irregular inner part of the pinna of the ear.

Canines: The two upper and two lower pointed teeth next to the incisors.

Carpals: Pastern joint bones.

Carp back: Arched back.

Castrate: To surgically remove the testicles of a male; to geld.

Champion: A dog that has won three Challenge Certificates under three different judges at Championship shows in the UK. In the USA the title is awarded on points won at major shows.

Chest: The body enclosed by the ribs.

Choke chain: A chain or leather collar fitted to the dog's neck in such a way that the amount of pressure exerted by hand tightens or loosens it. Also referred to as a check chain.

Collar: A circle of leather or chain used to direct and control the dog when the leash (lead) is attached.

Condition: Health of the dog, shown by coat, weight, appearance and deportment.

Conformation: Form and structure, make-up and shape of a dog; the arrangement of the parts in conformance with breed standard requirements.

Cow hocked: Hocks turned towards one another.

Crossbred: The progeny of purebred parents of different breeds.

Croup: The rear part of the back above the hind legs.

Cryptorchid: An adult dog whose testicles have not descended into the scrotum. A dog of this type cannot be exhibited.

Dam: The mother of a litter of puppies.

Dew claw: A claw on the inside of the leg, which is usually removed in early puppyhood but retained by some breeds.

Diagonals: Right front and left rear legs form the right diagonal; left front and right rear legs form the left diagonal. In the trot the diagonals move together.

Disqualify: A decision made by a judge or show committee, ruling that a dog has a condition making it ineligible for further competition under the dog show rules or under the *standard* for its breed.

Distemper teeth: Teeth marked, pitted, ringed and often stained, due to distemper or other severe infection.

Dock: To shorten the tail by cutting, usually done in early puppyhood if breed standards demand.

Dog show: An exhibition at which dogs are judged in accordance with an established standard of perfection for each breed.

Drive: A solid thrusting of the hind-quarters denoting sound locomotion.

Elbow: The upper arm and forearm joint.

Entropion: A condition in which the eyelid turns inward and the lashes irritate the eyeball.

Even bite: Meeting of upper and lower front teeth at edges with no overlap.

Expression: The general appearance of the front of the head, as typical of the breed.

Eye-teeth: The upper canines.

Fancier: Someone active in the sport of breeding, showing and judging purebred dogs.

Flank: The body area between the last rib and the hip.

Flat withers: An unattractive fault that is the result of short upright shoulder blades that abruptly join the withers.

Flews: Hanging upper lips, like those of a Bulldog, usually refers to the lateral parts of the lips.

Floating rib: The last, or 13th rib, which is unattached to other ribs of the rib-cage.

Flying trot: A fast gait in which all the feet are off the ground for a brief second during each half stride. Also called suspension trot.

Forearm: The foreleg bone between the elbow and the pastern.

Foreface: The front part of the head, before the eyes; the muzzle.

Foster mother: A bitch used to nurse another animal's whelps.

Front: The whole front part of the body.

Gait: A style of movement, e.g. running or trotting.

Groom: To brush, comb, trim and prepare a dog's coat for show or pleasure.

Handler: A person who handles (shows) a dog at dog shows, field trials, or obedience tests.

Haunches: Back part of the thigh on which the dog sits.

Haw: A third eyelid or nictitating membrane in the inside corner of the eye.

Heat: Seasonal period of the female, normally this occurs every six months.

Heel:	Command by handler to keep the dog close to his heel.	Pedigree:	Written record of the names of a dog's ancestors going back at least three generations.
Heel free:	Command whereby the dog must walk to heel without a lead.	Pencilling:	The dark lines on the surface of the toes in some breeds, notably the English Toy Terrier [Manchester Terrier (Toy)].
Height:	Dog's height measured from the ground to the top of the shoulder.	Points:	Colour correlated on face, ears, legs and tail – usually white, black or tan.
Hind-quarters:	Rear anatomy of dog (pelvis, thighs, hocks and paws).	Puppy:	A dog under one year old.
Hip dysplasia:	Malformation of the ball of the hip joint, usually hereditary.	Purebred:	A dog whose sire and dam belong to the same breed and are themselves of unmixed descent since the recognition of the breed.
Hocks:	Those joints in the hind limbs below the true knees, or stifle joints.		
Inbreeding:	Mating within the same family: a bitch to her sons, or a dog to his daughters.	Reach of front	Length of forward stride taken by forelegs without wasted or excessive motion.
Incisors:	The upper and lower front teeth, between the canines.	Register:	To record details of a dog's breeding with the respective Kennel Club.
In season:	In heat ready for mating.		
Ischium:	Hip bone.	Scapula:	The shoulder blade.
Kiss marks:	Tan spots on the coat on the cheeks and over the eyes.	Scissor bite:	A bite in which the upper front teeth slightly overlap the lower front teeth.
Lead:	A strap cord or chain attached to the collar or harness for the purpose of restraining or leading the dog: a leash.	Sire:	The father of a litter puppies.
		Smooth coat:	Short, sleek hair lying close to the skin.
Level back:	One that makes a straight line from withers to tail, but is not necessarily parallel to the ground.	Soundness:	The state of mental and physical health when all organs and faculties are functioning normally.
Level bite:	When the front teeth incisors of the upper and lower jaws meet edge to edge.	Spay:	The surgical removal (hysterectomy) of the bitch's reproductive organs to stop conception.
Licence:	Permission granted by the AKC to a non-member club to hold a dog show, or obedience test for field trial. In the UK, all shows in which purebred dogs are exhibited are held under Kennel Club licence.	Speak:	To bark.
		Splay feet:	Feet with toes spread wide.
		Spring of ribs:	Curvature of ribs for heart and lung capacity.
		Stance:	Manner of standing.
		Standard:	The standard of perfection for each breed.
Line breeding:	The mating of related dogs of the same breed, within the line, or family, to a common ancestor, e.g. a dog to his grand-dam.	Stifle:	That joint in the hind leg of a dog approximating to the knee in man, particularly relating to the inner side.
Loin:	The part of the body between the last rib and the back legs.	Stop:	The depression between and in front of the eyes, roughly corresponding to the bridge of the nose.
Match show:	An informal dog show at which no Championship points are awarded.		
		Straight hocks:	Hocks that are absolutely straight vertically.
Mate:	The breeding of dog and bitch.	Stud:	Male used for breeding.
Milk teeth:	First teeth. (Puppies lose these at 4–6 months.)	Stud book:	A record of the breeding particulars of recognized breeds.
Molars:	Dogs have two molars on each side of the upper jaw, and three on each side of the lower jaw. Upper molars have three roots, lower have two roots.		
		Topline:	The outline of the dog from behind the withers to the tail set.
		Trot:	A two-beat diagonal gait in which the feet at diagonally opposite ends of the body strike the ground together: right hind with left front and left hind with right front.
Muzzle:	The part of the head containing the mouth and nose. A device to prevent biting.		
Neck well set on:	Good neckline, merging with strong withers, forming a transition into topline.	Type:	The characteristic qualities distinguishing a breed, the embodiment of a standard.
Occiput:	Upper, back point of the skull		
Overhang:	A heavy or pronounced brow.	Undershot:	Having the lower jaw protecting the opposite of *overshot*.
Over-reaching:	Fault in the trot caused by more angulation and drive from behind than in front, so that the rear feet are forced to step to one side of the forefeet to avoid touching.	Upper arm:	The humerus or foreleg bone between the shoulder blade and the forearm.
		Vent:	Both the anal opening and the small area of light hair directly beneath the tail.
Overshot:	When the upper teeth project beyond the lower; also called pig jaw.		
Pads:	The tough, cushioned soles of the feet.	Whelping:	Giving birth to puppies.
		Whelps:	Newly born puppies.
Paper foot:	A flat foot with thin pads.	Withers:	The highest point of the shoulders, just behind the neck.
Pastern:	The region of the foreleg between the carpus (wrist) and the digits.	Wry mouth:	Mouth in which the lower jaw does not line up with the upper.
Peak:	A prominent occiput.		

Appendix II

Abbreviations

A.D.R.K.	Allgemeiner Deutscher Rottweiler Klub – General German Rottweiler Club
AI	Artificial insemination
AKC	American Kennel Club
ANKC	Australian National Kennel Club
AOC	Any other colour
AVNSC	Any Variety Not Separately Classified
B	Bitch
BIS	Best in Show
BOB	Best of Breed
BOS	Best Opposite Sex
CAC	Certificat d'aptitude au Championnat de Beauté
CACIB	Certificat d'aptitude au Championnat International de Beauté
CC	Challenge Certificate
CD	Companion Dog
CDEX	Companion Dog Excellent
Ch	Champion
CKC	Canadian Kennel Club
D	Dog
FCI	Federation Cynologique Internationale
Int Ch	International Champion
JW	Junior Warrant
KC	Kennel Club (UK)
LKA	Ladies Kennel Association
LOF	Livre des Origines Francais (French Stud Book)
LOSH	Livre Origines St Hubert (Belgian Stud Book)
NAF	Name applied for
Nordic Ch	Nordic Champion
OBCh	Obedience Champion
P	Puppy
PD	Police Dog
PV	Parvo virus
TD	Tracker Dog
UD	Utility Dog
UDEX	Utility Dog Excellent
WD	Working Dog

Useful Addresses

Kennel Clubs
Australia Australian National Kennel Council, Royal Show Grounds, Ascot Vale, Victoria
Belgium Societe Royale Saint-Hubert, Avenue de l'Armee 25, B-1040, Brussels
Canada Canadian Kennel Club, 2150 Bloor Street West, Toronto M6S 1M8, Ontario
France Societe Centrale Canine, 215 Rue St Denis, 75083 Paris, Cedex 02
Germany Verband f fur das Deutsche Hundewesen (VDH), Postfach 1390, 46 Dortmund
Holland Raad van Beheer op Kynologisch Gebied in Nederland, Emmalaan 16, Amsterdam, Z
Ireland Irish Kennel Club, 23 Earlsfort Terrace, Dublin 2
Italy Ente Nazionale Della Cinofilia Italiana, Viale Premuda, 21 Milan
New Zealand New Zealand Kennel Club, Private Bag, Porirua, New Zealand
Spain Real Sociedad Central de Fomento de las razas en Espana, Los Madrazo 20, Madrid 14
United Kingdom The Kennel Club, 1-4 Clarges Street, London W1Y 8AB
United States of America American Kennel Club, 51 Madison Avenue, New York, NY 10010; The United Kennel Club Inc, 100 East Kilgore Road, Kalamazoo, MI 49001-5598

General Addresses
The United Kingdom
The Agility Club The Spinney, Aubrey Lane, Redbourn, Hertfordshire AL3 7AN
British Small Animals Veterinary Association 7 Mansfield Street, London W1M 0AT
British Veterinary Association 7 Mansfield Street, London W1M 0AT
National Canine Defence League 1 Pratt Mews, London NW1 0AD
The Royal Society for the Prevention of Cruelty to Animals RSPCA Headquarters, Causeway, Horsham, Sussex RH12 1HG

The United States
American Animal Hospital Association 3612 East Jefferson, South Bend, Indiana 46615
American Society for the Prevention of Cruelty to Animals 441 East 92nd Street, New York 10028
American Veterinary Medical Association 930 North Meacham Road, Schaumburg, Illinois 60196
Orthopaedic Foundation for Animals 817 Virginia Avenue, Columbia, Missouri 65201

Rottweiler Clubs
Some Breed Clubs in Britain
The Rottweiler Club, Sec: Elizabeth Harrap. 'Pangora', Crays Pond Road, Goring Heath, Nr Reading, Berkshire British Rottweiler Assoc. Midland Rottweiler Club, Northern Rottweiler Club, Scottish Rottweiler Club, Welsh Rottweiler Club and Northern Ireland Rottweiler Club.

Addresses of secretaries of the above clubs can be obtained from the Kennel Club, 1-4 Clarges Street, London W1Y 8AB
Some Breed Clubs in America
American Rottweiler Club, Sec: Jody Engel, Box 560072, Miami, Florida 33256.
Colonial Rottweiler Club (Philadelphia), Medallion Rottweiler Club (Chicago), Golden State Rottweiler Club (Los Angeles), Western Rottweiler Owners (California), Houston Bay Area Rottweiler Club (Texas), Texas Rottweiler Club, Orange Coast Rottweiler Club (California), Tidewater Rottweiler Club (Virginia). Addresses of secretaries of the above clubs can be obtained from the American Kennel Club, 51, Madison Avenue, New York, NY 10010

Other Rottweiler Clubs
Australia: Rottweiler Club of Victoria,
Rottweiler Club of South Australia
Canada: The Rottweiler Club of
Canada
New Zealand: Central Rottweiler Club
Inc

Further Reading
Breed Books
The Complete Rottweiler, Muriel,
Freeman, Howell Book House, USA
All About the Rottweiler, Mary
Macphail, Pelham Books, London
The Rottweiler, Midland Rottweiler
Club, UK
The Rottweiler, Dr Dogmar Hodinar,
Von Palisaden Publications, USA
Training
Training Your Dog, the step-by-step
manual. Volhard & Fisher, Howell
Book House, USA
The Agility Dog, Peter Lewis, Canine
Publications, UK
Training Your Dog, Joan Palmer,
Salamander Books Ltd, London 1986
General
Practical Dog Breeding and Genetics,
Eleanor Frankling, Popular Dogs,
London
The Conformation of the Dog, R H
Smyth, Popular Dogs, London
Canine Terminology, H Spira, Harper
& Row, Sydney

Above: *Properly socialized and well-
trained, your Rottweiler should be a
companion to be cherished.*

Understanding Your Dog, Michael W
Fox, The Anchor Press Ltd, UK
Dog Steps, R P Elliot, Howell Book
House, New York
All About Your Dog's Health, GP West,
Pelham Books, London
Understanding Your Dog, PR
Messent, Quarto Publishing, London
First Aid For Pet Animals, BM Bush,
A&C Black, UK.

Magazines
The United Kingdom
The Kennel Gazette, 1-5 Clarges
Street, Piccadilly, London W1Y 8AB.
Dog World, 9 Tufton Street, Ashford,
Kent TN23 1QN.
Our Dogs, Oxford Road, Station
Approach, Manchester.
Dogs Monthly, Unit One, Bowen
Industrial Estate, Aberbargoed,
Bargoed, Mid-Glamorgan, CF8 9ET.

The United States
Dog World Magazine, 300 West
Adams Street, Chicago, Il 60606.
*Pure-Bred Dogs/American Kennel
Gazette*, 51 Madison Avenue, New
York, NY 10010.